OF RUSSIA: A YEAR INSIDE

BRENT ANTONSON

PROUDLY PUBLISHED BY:

planksip

Publisher: 0722401 BC Ltd dba. planksip® Publishing

Victoria, BC Canada

www.planksip.org

Library and Archives Canada Cataloguing in Publication

Versions

Hardcover: 978-1-77443-075-0

Electronic: 978-1-77443-074-3

Paperback: 978-1-77443-073-6

Cover

Cover Image: Альфия Шайхулова (Alfia Shaikhulova)

Background words are from Andrei Platonov, a Soviet Russian novelist, short story writer, philosopher, playwright, and poet.

Design in collaboration with planksip®.

Portions of this work appeared previously in Russian translation in a Voronezh newspaper and in the magazine Vancouver Russia.

"I cannot forecast to you the action of Russia. It is a riddle wrapped in a mystery inside an enigma."
— *Sir Winston Churchill*

"There is no mind of Russia; Russia just believes there is."
— *Anya*

This book is dedicated to my parents; those two special people who gave me roots, wings, and used my five year-old-body to smuggle a souvenir bullet out of the Soviet Union in 1974.
God Bless 'em

CONTENTS

FOREWORD

When we talk about travelling, we often speak of landscapes, culture, food, and people. Yet, the real essence of a journey is not the places we visit but the stories we uncover and the lessons we learn along the way. *Of Russia: A Year Inside* by Brent Antonson is a testament to this truth. As I pen this foreword, I feel privileged to introduce you to Antonson's riveting exploration of Russia, a land of paradoxes, a narrative that's as beautiful as it is heart-wrenching. Revealed through a mutual friend's YouTube channel, Bernie Chats, I encourage you to watch the episode, *I was tortured by authorities in Russia!*

Brent Antonson, an English language teacher by profession, ventured into Russia not as a mere tourist but as an observer, a learner, a participant. His dedication to understanding and respecting the diversity and profundity of the country he chose to call home for a year is evident on every page of this book. However, his journey, deeply intertwined with the people, places, and language of Russia, had an abrupt and violent ending that leaves an indelible mark on his tale.

Antonson recounts the chilling events that led to his forced departure from Russia in this book. The brutal attack by

Russian police, a testament to the nation's dark underbelly, serves as a sad reminder of the harsh realities that sometimes hide beneath the surface of a beautiful country rich in history and culture. Despite the tragedy he experienced, Antonson's narrative remains as much a testament to the resilience of the human spirit as it is a compelling exploration of Russian life and culture.

What distinguishes *Of Russia: A Year Inside* is Antonson's ability to balance the dark and the light, the bitter and the sweet. His love for the Russian people, and the friendships he cultivates shines through, even as he recounts the painful experiences that cut his journey short. It's this juxtaposition that makes his narrative so engaging, so poignant, so real.

Our world is woven with stories—some beautiful, some painful, and many a mix of both. This is a story that deserves to be told and heard. I feel honored to have found this book and to share it with you.

So, prepare yourself to embark on a journey that goes beyond the borders of countries and delves into the heart of what it means to be human, what it means to connect with others, what it means to love a place, and what it means to endure. Brent Antonson is your guide, and Russia, in all its beauty and paradox, is your destination. As you turn the pages of *Of Russia: A Year Inside*, remember every story, every relationship, has it's light and dark. It's up to us to listen, learn, and carry the lessons forward.

Let the journey begin.

Daniel Sanderson
— planksip® Founder and CEO, philosopher, and publisher.

A CANADIAN SUMMER

I accepted a position teaching English to Russians with the *Institute of Law and Economics* starting in September and through to the January break. That school was in the Russian city of *Voronezh*, an eleven hour train shuffle south of Moscow. And Voronezh is on the River Don. That's all I knew since the internet and large travel bible had little information. Certainly there wasn't enough data to decide if moving to Voronezh was worthwhile. But I sensed it was.

I had seldom had an entire room's eyes on me. I wasn't even sure I was prepared for people looking at me for instruction for an hour let alone many hours a day for months. My DNA is littered with stage-fright genes. At 31, the age when the mind no longer wonders about running off to the army or the circus, I was faced with a life altering option of travel by teaching. It seems I was singled out by evolutionary forces to wander this little globe curious, losing puzzle pieces. I was armed with a recognized teaching certificate and there was a little Russian in my frontal lobes from the Trans-Siberian journey I had taken with my father and brother three years prior. All was in order.

I wanted to learn 'Russian', not just penetrate the thick opaqueness of the language enough to buy cigarettes, but feel what it's like to communicate informally in the dominant tongue of 300 million people. I wanted to be intimate in the ability. I wanted to curse in Russian; I wanted to pray in Russian. For that I needed to be immersed in it. Teaching English in Russia would afford that. Russia, financially, could not. Part of the investment required me to cover my own costs to Moscow. I was not going to Russia for a paycheque, though. Instead Russia would afford me a view, in-depth and personal, into her world and workings and things a paycheque couldn't provide.

The teaching and learning would, I presumed, be enlightening trade-offs. When I was searching for places to ply my new trade, I resisted cities with an expat community. Prague, Bangkok, and Shanghai, while captivating, weren't on my list. I needed a place to call my own - not hints, tricks, and dining tips from Donald 'the lonely roommate whose parents think he is still attending Michigan State'. I wanted to be deep in Russia, and stayed away from busy Moscow campuses and hectic Saint Petersburg colleges, and found a simple online posting for a teacher needed in a small city in the south. I wanted to be *Zhivago*.

Russia has long amazed me. Having spent traveller's-time in the Soviet Union, Siberia, Estonia, and passing through similar experiments in economics, politics, and you-never-know-who's-listening countries, I had a childlike curiosity toward the parallel lives lived behind that Cold War frontier of silence. What are Russians really like? How does a single day play out in a small city? Are there still bread queues? Is life really all that different after the collapse of the USSR? Does Aeroflot recognize Airmiles? The steady slide of the Soviet Union's demise from a superpower was like watching the Titanic leave port. And I wanted to be onboard.

I longed to be among the Russians; perhaps even secretly to be one. Canada, for all her first-world membership credentials, doesn't shine like a country from outside her borders. It's just there, taking up map. It's the *idea* of Canada that sells it. But our nationalism is saturated with doubt. Her appeal is to rich foreigners, hopeful immigrants, and people who want to smoke pot and marry someone of the same sex. I was too Canadian, too apathetic and indifferent to the life it afforded. In Russia, I would be a foreigner until I felt one to my home and native land.

I do love Canada; enough to let her go.

A RUSSIAN AUTUMN

I was a learner. I was not a teacher. Moscow's *Shereme-tyevo* Airport met my plane hours on beneath a bosom of grey clouds. As the plane slapped the runway, economy class passengers broke into a whistling frenzy and peanuts were thrown about. From the last window in the Airbus A319 I watched my backpack get thrown onto an airport cart. The zipper had split; a wool sock hung out in surrender. I feared my laptop would break over the ground in small fragments of what the KGB would call exhibits A through Ж. A large titanium case filled with all sorts of heavy titanium things was thrown on top. Then the sound equipment from a German rock band landed atop that. My belongings would now be last off the wagons and the final pieces to the Claims Area.

I wound my watch eleven time zones from Vancouver. The flight was late. I stood in the same bottleneck Customs queue where I had stood a few years before when my brother Sean, Dad, and I set off on the Trans-Siberian railway. Other than evidence it had been swept a time or two, the entire hall was a duplication of that slow socializing process. The same light bulbs were burnt out. The same pungent odors leaked from sweaty Russians. I was sure that the same cold-shoulder immigration agent called me up to the window. She reminded me of my uncle. I was in.

Alexander had travelled from Voronezh, Southern Russia, to fetch me. He'd spent a night on a train and doubtlessly crossed many a subway station. I asked how I would recognize him and had only been told that he would be wearing a yellow suit. This conjured up bizarre images, none of which would turn out true. I was anxious to meet him, to befriend my new boss, and become comrades in a war called education. His final email said he would be holding a cardboard sign that said 'Brent Antonson' (it would be the last time I would see my name spelt correctly). I felt special, needed, accepted. Scanning a massive gathering of leather-capped taxi drivers, each hoisting a cardboard sign, I saw Alexander, grinning in a suit I never grew to like.

He wasn't Russian to look at really. None of his features seemed indigenous. We were both 31 years old and 5' 11". Alexander had a sandy blond part that had overgrown his high forehead. Moist patches on his face and under his armpits indicated he'd been in the tight crowd for some time. My delays took two hours off any plans Alexander had in mind. He was welcoming, yet preoccupied with leaving. It was getting dark and it was implied that I was the cause of it. Russia runs on its own time. Three standard minutes seems like one long Russian minute.

The airport is a congested forty-minute drive from downtown Moscow, and from the back of a crowded mini-bus, I learned, through his broken English, about my new boss. And he learned about me. He was married with a young daughter. I was single and here for dashes of romance. No one in his family had ever owned a car. I owned two, one for parts. He'd never been anywhere other than Voronezh and Moscow. I'd travelled around the globe once. I couldn't discern if we were to be friends, colleagues or if I was an expensive subordinate until my visa expired. Every time I said something I felt as though I'd imparted evidence that would be used against me. I sensed he was a dog person who'd been raised with cats. Perhaps he was still miffed about Canadian Paul Henderson's goal over the Russians in 1972. Russians have been known to harbour grudges for decades. Alexander didn't know what to make of my question. He didn't follow hockey, he said. With all my Canadian heart, though, I liked him.

A little later we were jettisoned into an open span of asphalt where hundreds of people and a gaggle of taxis were sitting in the dark. The cause for his hasty welcome became apparent. Alexander hadn't been to this immense city of eleven million in a long time. He was intimidated. I had, ironically, been there since he had. Moscow in an unfamiliar night is a challenge to a stranger. We had to make our way to the hotel and this required two further transfers in taxi-buses.

Russians use their names differently from North Americans. They use patronymics; that is, their father's first name becomes their middle name with a conjugation. Thus, through some linguistic alchemy, Alexander became *Sasha* which was a pleasant, informal and non-confrontational use of Alexander Michailovitch's name. He advised me of this early on. Sasha, as he now was known to me, had prepared the train tickets and accommodations in advance to make my welcome successful. Our one night reservation was in the empty *Palomnicheskij* Hotel. It sat near Moscow's State University of the Russian Federation. Our train to Voronezh would leave the following night.

I marveled over the Cyrillic script on the hotel rules while Sasha negotiated the check-in with a woman who looked like she'd been raised in the dark. She tapped her watch as if to say we were late. Sasha mumbled something and they both looked over to me. Our punishment was a small room. When my luggage arrived and was parked, we lost the floor. As a book lover, school supply hoarder, and oh-the-Russians-will-love-this-as-a-gift things, I'd brought with me more unnecessary stuff than anything else. The result of my excesses was four pieces of scuffed luggage that weighed in at eighty kilograms. Two pieces had wheels. Due to our hurry, Sasha had struggled with two.

'Thank the gods for the wheel, eh?' I said, chuckling in defense.

'Would you care for a walk to the university?' Sasha asked as though he'd broken the silence.

I hadn't slept in days and weighed my answer with thoughts about slipping into a coma. As I poised to decline, I remembered that the State University of the Russian Federation was likely a Mecca of Russian education, a cathedral of sorts. Refusing could jeopardize my professional cover. I did not want to go.

'What a super, super idea,' I replied with a saint-like beam.

Moscow University is a *vysotki*; one of seven massive gothic skyscrapers that Stalin had built during his 'I am *sooo* not envious of New York' phase. Restorations to the scholastic contribution to the skyline were being endured, and a mess of scaffolding clung around it. Two men with semi-automatic Kalashnikovs thwarted our attempt at the front doors, leading me to conclude that men with assault rifles were guarding schools. Sasha led me off on a leaf-strewn path beyond the university, down forested trails, to an overlook where Moscow fell into view. We were miles from the Kremlin core and lights scorched into the horizon. The stars above were faint in Moscow's luminous bath; dramatic shadows lurked around the suburbs. Sasha pointed out the Ostenkino TV tower and the Spartak stadium. The view was a hang-out for lovers, bored taxi drivers, and drunk Russians talking to themselves.

Sasha and I walked back to our little room and rearranged my luggage. I sat in bed and wrote on my laptop until the hotel shut off the electricity. Then I smoked duty-free Marlboros in thought about where I was and where I was headed. Russian snores emanated from beyond the wall of luggage. Sasha, my new friend, was sleeping. Everything seemed to be going right.

We entered into a beautiful morning with high hopes of making the most of a day in the city. By the network of Moscow's massive subway infrastructure, Sasha and I made it to the Kremlin environs and tracked down a McDonald's near the Bolshoi theatre. I treated my new boss to a meal of sorts he'd never experienced. He had heard of McDonald's, that elusive trademark of capitalism, but there were none to be found south of Moscow.

'I may actually have to learn how to cook,' I said to myself.

'You don't know how to cook?'

'I said that to myself Sasha.'

'Oh,' he seemed happy to drop the subject.

'So what'll it be?' I pushed him into the excitement. 'Look at that menu… look at those pictures! A specter is haunting you - the specter of choice!'

'I think the Royal Cheeseburger looks quite good,' he said, overwhelmed.

'Hey, does the KGB eat at McDonald's?' I asked.

'There is no KGB anymore, it is the FSB,' he said.

'I don't think Hollywood knows that. What does FSB stand for?'

'*Federalnaya Sluzhba Bezopasnosti…*' Sasha enunciated.

'Do they eat at McDonald's?' I asked. 'What about Communists? Or the Mafia, I bet they eat at McDonald's… they probably *own* McDonald's… picture this: 'The McMafia introduces a new burger to the menu: *the McXtortion.*'

'Where did you say you got your education?'

'Sash...' I said.

'Sasha. It is Sasha. Don't make me go back to Alexander.'

We walked against the foot traffic on the busy side-roads and wrapped back along the riverfront. Eddies of leaves spun in the Moskva's flow. I held the handrail tightly and looked downwind, down the mighty Moskva River. It was like a hug from an old friend. Adjacent to us and across a suicidal wall of traffic sat the *Rossiya* hotel; at 3300 rooms it is the largest in Europe and the object most likely to be in the background of any Moscow postcard. We approached St. Basil's basilica at the foot of Red Square by an underground walkway.

The skirt of history around this square is responsible for the face of Eurasia. The Kremlin, fortified in turrets atop a castle wall, has given shape to the world, for good or ill, since the Dark Ages. That era is no more apparent than in Saint Basil's, that familiar radish-domed church that pokes its golden crosses towards Mir. Six hundred years ago, the church, commissioned for a victory, was completed. Rumours abound that the structure was so superb and unique that Ivan the Terrible had the architect's eyes spooned out to prevent further replications. It is by the will of God that Stalin's oppression of religion didn't level the basilica and build something more boxy.

Idolatry was tolerated only when directed to the opiate of the state. Hence, Lenin's tomb sat snug against the Kremlin. Lenin's deified remains, which have filled Red Square with pilgrimages, were open. I had never had the opportunity to see Lenin; the few times I'd tried to see him, he was not to be disturbed. Lenin was a powerful and controversial leader and I had respect for his courage, foresight and nerve, and I thought seeing his corpse might establish some dialogue with the past. Sasha asked a police officer where the line began and was told that after we'd stored our cameras at a security shack three-quarters of a mile away, we could queue off the square where the militsia were bringing groups of fifty beyond the small edifice to see Lenin's tomb.

'You know, Sasha, Lenin could be safely left outside in Moscow nine months a year. I mean the man is now all about Celsius right?'

Sasha didn't acknowledge me as we entered the tomb. You are not allowed to talk when you enter. You can't even ask why you can't talk or AK-47s will be waved in your face, you'll be treated to Russian grimaces and you still won't get an answer. Lenin was under heavy guard. Soldiers stood at each corner, eyeing everyone, suspecting everyone. Maybe it was respect or perhaps it was history's longest wake or maybe they didn't want anyone stapling the new constitution to Lenin's forehead. It was dark as we dropped twelve stairs to the bottom. The line wove up a few steps and around a stage where the 120 year-old man lay. Lenin isn't looking well these days; more like a Mattel action figure than the Communist leader ultimately responsible for a lack of Slurpee machines in the Motherland. Seeing Lenin's grave is a Russian responsibility though it is rumoured he may be buried underground, finally ending the Russian leader's 70 years as a taxidermied has-been. Besides, then he could roll over in his grave.

Behind Lenin's mausoleum, the guards diverted the group through the necropolis against the Kremlin wall. Stalin remains there (though probably not as deep as many would like). Lenin's wife, Soviet political figures and American John Reed rest in the shade of Lenin. It is some morbid real estate.

In a quiet city dusk, we spotted the golden domes of Christ the Savior, a church recently restored to its pre-Soviet look. The massive central dome was polished enough that God, should He want, could see Himself. Night fell swiftly upon us, prompting a haphazard return to the hotel for our luggage. We hailed a taxi for *Pavelyetskaya* station.

Our train eased in to its track on time. The rugged front looked worn and tough, even proud. Russian trains have an appeal that transcends their functionality. There is romance, travel and possibilities. They are relegated to the task of carrying a country's people to places they've saved up for years to visit. The railway is a big part of Russian culture. Our ride was eleven hours. The time of departure would get us into Voronezh well-rested the next morning. My excitement, my wonder at the train as a supreme entity, seemed lost on Sasha. It wasn't attractive or stupendous to him; it was the way to travel home - just a long ride. The train is so much a part of Russian lives that they've lost 'touch' with things Westerners might find charismatic. As the carriage attendant flipped her thick thumb through our boarding passes, I told Sasha I felt that there wasn't enough time in Canada to take the train. Our lives are too fast and a train is too slow. Maybe he understood me or maybe he was being polite. He said 'Ah'.

We made it to our berth and found two men stretched out reading the daily periodicals. I smiled as Sasha told them we were going to renovate the room in order to fit my luggage. It was like a big game of Tetris trying to arrange everything, and the moment the last piece fell into place, the train nudged away from the station. I ran to the windows in the hall and caught serenity in the shrinking skyline. Moscow was rolling off, Voronezh was now inevitable.

Due to jetlag, I spent a lot of the night staring at the ceiling. Just when I was about to fall asleep, I spotted light running beneath the cotton drape. Sunrise on the train's east side lit up the railway ties, a covering of frost, and sleepy villages. The orange orb threw autumnal colours through the birch forests. Trees sided the track in a uniform density broken by paths that sniveled off to the shadows.

Trains in Russia are comforting in the morning, particularly train number 25, the 'Moscow—Voronezh', because the destination is reached at eight a.m. Men are usually holding their heads, scratching, and suffering from any over-indulgence hours before. Women tend to noisy children and packing. There is little conversation about the compartments as people take unsympathetically long turns in the only open washroom. All one could do was wait and rock gently to the rhythm of the carriage.

A small village spilt from the tracks. Stiff wood fences railed off gardens and divided dachas. For all the foreignness beyond the window, all the anticipatory angst, I felt a calm when a slicing grey horizon moved towards the train. From the maps I'd studied, this was *the* river. The massive River Don snuggled up to a final turf of village and fired a murky tributary beneath a riveted bridge. The far bank opposed us a few miles away, messing up the east side of the Don with its grey apartment blocks. Known innovatively as *The Left Bank*, Sasha pointed out that it is across from the city core which is where I would be living. Sasha, indeed most people I would ever meet, lived on the 'residential' Left Bank in right-angle apartment slabs, built up from the shore in cartons of concrete.

Voronezh was rather unnoticeably arrived at. The city didn't scenically reveal itself in a bend of the tracks or jumble above a hill beside us. Beneath the train window, a city quickly grew from a rustic village of wooden homes. A platform began pacing the wagon in the shadow of a tall iron fence. It was a graceful maneuver to the last wheeze of the airbrakes. I looked out the window and sighed. I had made it.

Sasha pointed out Marina, divinely sculpted into a black trench coat, standing near the gates beneath a black umbrella. Her thin lips parted as she watched the busy windows of the carriage. We waddled my luggage to the door and she pulled Sasha down a step, smiling in Russian. Sasha introduced Marina as my colleague, a Russian English teacher who had taught Russian in Britain. Marina, who commanded her English with high profile idioms, embraced my hand and chose the smallest piece of luggage to haul to a car. I immediately judged her as depression meets Goth meets rural Russia. The three of us dragged ourselves towards an idling Lada that sat over a puddle. Autumn was playing in the air, rousing the cumuli into dark showers. The driver climbed away from his cigarette and mild music to wrestle my belongings into the trunk. I managed a challenged smile as he cursed through their organization. Once loaded, we merged into the Voronezhian rush-hour.

Lawless Ladas raced about the laneless streets, trams paced crumbled sidewalks and people shuffled into old buildings. Concrete, the essential Russian building material, was adorned with old, faded advertising. Slabs of it were strewn anywhere in the preformed blocks used for apartments. Voronezh was built lengthwise along a main thoroughfare. I would learn the boulevard to be *Koltsovskaya*, one of three main avenues that triangle the city. My lodgings would be on this street. Marina broke away from her discussion with Sasha in a bid to understand Canada, 'I looked up Canada on the internet and saw the national sport is lacrosse, not hockey as I believed.'

'Lacrosse is… lacrosse.' I said wringing my fists. 'No, ask

any patriot in Canada and they'll say hockey and basketball are Canadian. The States can have baseball, Bush and apple pie. The NBA destroyed a very good Canadian game using peach baskets nailed to walls. There were no salary caps, union strikes or Americans involved. But that's America; they took 12-cent fruit baskets and replaced them with $12,000 backboards that no little kid in rural Ontario is going to earn picking peaches.'

'… do you play lacrosse?' she asked in her spicy accent.

'No one really does… I think its status is a concession we made to…'

'To whom?' she asked.

'I don't mean to correct you, but it is *to who*,' I imparted.

'No, it is *to whom*,'

'Ok. Well, hockey and basketball are Canadian.'

'How many basketball teams does Canada have?' she pressed.

'Well, that is irrelevant. You are implying that there is a correlation between…y'know, I see where this is going... are we there yet?'

'Is it true Canadians club baby seals?'

'Wha-' I figured that would surface, just not within minutes after arriving. 'Ok, there are a few archaic laws and stupid peo-…in a word, no. But if you want to talk about our human rights record… nuclear safety or maybe even why our soldiers are called 'Peacekeepers'…'

'We is here!' Sasha interrupted as the car slowed to a stop.

We were only five minutes of traffic into our airtight drive when we arrived at my building. I stepped into the vertigo of my new 'home'. It rose five stories and was wounded with time. The L-shape bent it off the main street and wrapped it into a patch of rough driveway. A long wooden bench with a few elderly men playing cards sat in a small garden of dead weeds and laundry lines.

At the main steel door which led to the apartments above, we punched a small metal keypad numerous times to ensure I knew how the system worked. I pushed a metal knob below the painted number 2, then the faded 4, then the missing 6 and hooked a finger over a sharp latch. The metal door quivered open with a groan. Inside, beyond the fuzz of light from the door, it was dark. One flight of stairs climbed to a small landing with four bulletproof-era doors choked by the light of a dim bulb. Marina fumbled through a fist of keys and stabbed three locks. The peephole was two feet lower than my ocular height. So was the neighbour's. Sasha made a grab for the keys but was told something in stern Russian that made him stop and slink down to the car for the last of my bags. The door opened to a hallway. My eyes followed the wood paneling around to a hideous Siberian death mask jutting out of the wall.

'Outside of a very, very bad omen,' I said, 'What the hell is that?'

Sasha stepped forward and swung the mask out, revealing the whirring power meter and four porcelain fuse holders. I would never be comfortable with the fuse box; it would glare at me every time I entered the flat. It had Russian screws and I was without a Russian screwdriver. The mask would stay there throughout my time in Voronezh, attracting questions, watching people remove their footwear, and killing libidos.

The living room was furnished in early seventies décor in a country that had a different 'seventies' from most. Carpets hung off the walls. The furniture was all the same drab colour. The desk, the bookshelves, the dresser and the garbage can were all part of a set.

As I walked across the room I clipped my head on a chandelier and knocked loose some 200 tiny prisms. (This chandelier would suffer nine such events in my time in Voronezh. It took forty-five sober minutes to replace them all. After the ninth time I would consign them to a drawer.)

I raced to the window to see my view. Across from my second-storey flat, through a tangle of tram wires, sat the largest shopping attraction in town, the *Russia State Department Store*. Huddled at its doors was a cluster of kiosks, perhaps fifty of them. My location was already appreciated as an outstanding feature. I didn't have to take three trams and a taxi-bus to get a belt buckle, yard of fabric, or litre of 6% milk. A tram rumbled by, breaking any conversation until it'd passed. Hmm, I thought.

Marina showed me to my bedroom and waited by the door. In the strained light of a polyester drape I patted the depression in my bed, opened empty drawers, then went for the kitchen. It was small, with no microwave nor room for it should it be invented or imported. Well, I guess I won't be learning how to cook, I thought. There was a four foot fridge, a table for one and a Formica countertop that ran into a tiny sink. The small gas stove looked eager to throttle off to the floors above if ignited. Marina picked up an aged kettle with a floral design on it.

'Don't drink the water without boiling it first.'

'Why?'

'Don't drink the water without boiling it first.'

'Is that because-'

'Don't drink the water without boiling it first.'

'Ok.'

Marina dipped her chest onto my counter and peered into the bottom of a large metal container on the wall.

'Ok Brant... the gas. This feature is likely to take time to adapt to. Take notes, draw pictures, fuse synapses.'

'I'm rather slow when it comes to fast things,' I said.

Marina looked back to the counter and repeated the methodic sequence of valves, dials and matchsticks until she was sure I'd survive it alone. Then I took notes as she walked me through bathing procedures:

1. Turn on hot water tap in the bathroom. That starts gas flowing in kitchen.
2. Run to kitchen while striking match.
3. Approach area where gas is likely to have seeped to, and extend arm.
4. Once enveloped in flame, return to bathtub, disrobe and jump in.
5. Don't touch the cold tap because that turns off the gas.
6. Should the gas go out, you'll know because the water goes cold (go to step #2 cold and nude).
7. Enjoy bathing, use the handheld shower with its six hose leaks.
8. Climb out and run to turn off the gas.
9. Return and turn off the water.

Sasha had been on the orange phone in the hallway, notifying someone that I had arrived. I looked over his shoulder at the rotary-dial. I hadn't considered bringing a phone. In fact none of the numerous travel checklists I'd ever seen suggested it. He looked up at me, smiled and hung up.

The two of them offered a final welcome then bade me my first *dosvydanias* and left me alone to settle with the jetlag that had been affecting my sentence structure. I watched the door close, sighed with my hands on my hips and swiveled to the death mask. In strides to the window, I ducked at the chandelier and confirmed I wasn't dreaming. A tram drudged by, shaking the whole apartment. Then I went to bed at noon.

It was dark when I woke. The lights were out. I did not know where I was. What woke me was a massive explosion. Then another. My brain turned into soup. I groped my way out of bed while frightened babble fell from my lips. I was in the invisible world of instinct. There was a chorus line of firearms. I dropped to the floor then reached up for the light switch. When I flipped it, nothing happened and I knew I was in Russia. I pulled my way to the window. The Chechnyans had moved into town. I crawled on my stomach to the phone and called Marina at midnight to alert her.

Then I saw purple sparkles silhouetting the low skyline. Marina laughed at my suspicions and told me Voronezh's football team had just beat Kazakhstan.

'The Fukels have won,' she said.

'Really,' I asked, 'The Fukels?'

'Yes,' she answered and said I could expect such phenomena with every local win.

'Marina, if you hadn't answered the phone, I'd be live on CNN by now.'

The phone rang at two am. I understood that a man wanted 'Lena'. They didn't understand me explaining in plain English with the occasional Russian word that she wasn't here and they hung up. Two hours later the phone rang again, with the same voice asking for Lena. It was four in the morning so I said *ona speet c'menye*, 'she's sleeping with me'. That really pissed him off. I suddenly hoped he didn't know the secret 2-4-6 security code to get in the building. I went to the door and made sure all three locks were secure. I bent down and looked out the peep-hole. For the first of many, many times I took the receiver off its plastic orange cradle. This act would perplex those who got a busy signal when they called. 'A telephone is sacred and potent device, you can't just leave the phone off the hook' they seemed to say. 'We had to wait four years for a phone. It is not a toy.'

Wrapping myself in towels, I prepared to have a bath. Following Marina's list of gas instructions, I turned the valve and struck a match. There were ten peculiar seconds then a flash of light so powerful I met God. Though I persevered for a half-hour, losing towels as I ran between the kitchen and bathroom to swivel one tap or another, I failed trying to get hot water. By then I was too scared to smoke or sleep because the flat smelled of gas.

The following day it was imperative that I get online. I had to confirm to friends and family that I had made it to point 'B'. Marina and I went to the only internet provider and in return for signing a contract agreeing to pay $1.57 per hour, I acquired an eight digit username, 12 digit identity logon, a 16 digit password and a 13 digit dedicated number.

The first complication was the rotary phone setup. I had to cut three wires, splice in a new plug and snake forty feet of wire around the room to the desk because it was far too heavy to move. Within a few hours I was able to find out where to put the Russian password and dial-up numbers. My laptop stuttered and connected itself, dropped the line and re-dialed. On the fourth attempt, my email home slowly left Russia.

And so I learned about my Russian home. The doorbell to my flat sounded like voltage being applied to the testes of a small rodent. The first time someone used it, I wept. It was such a fearsome sound that soon I had it modified with mittens, hair gel and duct tape. The toilet wouldn't swallow a cigarette butt. Water, electricity and gas seemed to be fickle commodities that came only when someone down the street decided to press a button or turn a valve. The building, like most, was warmed by central heating. This is a boiler in the basement that runs hot water through the apartments, spilling heat from radiators in each room. However, central heating for the entire city of Voronezh doesn't kick in until October 15th every year. Until then it is what Marina called 'sweater time'. The bathtub and sink share a swivel tap. There was no shower; bathing was the only option. I have preferred showering to bathing all my life. Bathing is so slow. I whined. I wrote some Haiku poetry about adapting as a cockroach scurried across the sink and dove under the bathtub. My eyebrows inverted. Cockroaches? The old-style tub itself was raised off the ground by small bathtub legs. I grabbed a homemade twig broom from the kitchen and swept it beneath the tub, disturbing dust, a bloody knife and two roach motels. I swept it all back under.

Dusty trams travelled the double set of tracks outside my window every few minutes. The entire building, wall units, lamps and doors shook every time. Some even made you blink uncontrollably. It took a week until I got used to them passing. On the plus side there was 24-hour transit. The flat was on the second of five storeys. At street level was an appliance dealer. My bedroom sat over the stereo section. For much of each day their music broke the concentration barrier, peaking at deafening volumes. I used earplugs with success until one went missing. I cut the remaining plug in half and that worked until one got stuck. Then I gave up.

I could hear a woman crying through the wall at night. In my entire time at the flat I would not run into her on the stairs or leaving her apartment. It perplexed me, and I waited to hear yelling or crashing that would prompt me to knock on her door and solve her abusive husband's problem with a Russian mallet. But there was nothing more than sobs and I could only wonder.

Marina had only recently joined the Institute but had taught English regularly for eight years elsewhere in the city. She had the task of helping me adjust to Voronezh and find the major and minor landmarks. I considered myself a person who could easily adapt to change and one that could enjoy getting lost. But Marina was strict and sensitive to her duties, and felt responsible to press me with a map and pen so any careless wandering wouldn't be blamed on her.

I had to buy a host of foods and cleaning supplies. I have an unspoken motto that instead of making things dirty, I economize and rarely use much. Nevertheless it was Marina who told me that my laundry would be done in the bathtub and I should have the appropriate cleanser.

'I'm sorry, did you just say…?'

Marina encouraged me to buy twelve rolls of coloured toilet paper simply because a shipment had just arrived from Poland and may not be repeated this season.

'I'm still confused. Did you say laundry/bathtub? I have suits.'

As for food, my one 'fear' of living in Russia was that I would not adapt well to fish, borscht, or strange-content-perogies as I was quite unadventurous when it came to trying new foods. However, I was able to enjoy the finest bread in Russia, if not the world, because the provincial territory of Voronezh was the black soil region, the bread basket of Russia. I found a meat that had the attributes of beef jerky and I located a cheese that rivaled anything I had ever had. Combined, I had the perfect meal for months on end. I called it the 'Russian Sub'. Marina insisted on bruised fruits and a handful of hitherto unknown legumes but these only wilted on my counter. When I told her that I fancied specific vegetables, Marina said she grew them at her parents dacha and that she would bring me armloads of garlic, radishes, and jelly jars of preserves.

With the immediate needs purchased and stored in my flat, Marina and I walked the city for two days. The Church of the Shroud owned a principal vista atop the cliffs above the river. It had a great bell in its high tower. I lived a few kilometres away but could hear the solemn knells on Sundays. I have longed for church bells to be a part of my Sunday mornings. Maybe it's because I grew up with sirens. But like foghorns or train whistles, church bells touch something deep within the skin, perhaps duty or dreams. Bells could be heard across the city from its tiny churches.

Inside the wide wooden doors, the church's walls seemed to close in. The ceiling was low and the interior was dark, typical of Russian churches. The light came from hundreds of candles that had been lit for the dead. There were small round stands filled with wax and candles of varying height. The murals and frescoes of Christ, Mary, and the saints were antiquated, stunning with their detail and made you take a step back in awe. Old Cyrillic script wove prayers around the dome. There was a lofty steeple above the pulpit that carried faint external light through stained glass windows. Entering a Russian church is more than a physical affair; you can feel your soul checking in.

The first time I went into the church, Marina took off her scarf and covered her head with it as is required for women, and I put out my cigarette in what I truly thought was an ashtray. We entered and stood among a few hundred people, for there were no seats. The highest priest exited a bank of golden doors and began to sway his incense. He was joined by other monks. They began chanting as they weaved through the crowd. There were tears by the dozens. Old women crossed their chests and clenched their white-knuckled fists. I was deeply moved.

Not far from the landmark church was the Wedding Bridge.

This small leap across a road held high significance to all Voronezhians. After a wedding, the groom would carry his bride the distance of the bridge. Then bottles of champagne and vodka would be consumed, then smashed in the hopes of a long life together. The bridge was old, withered by the centuries and constructed of rough stone. There were countless shards of glass and ribbons of bottle labels strewn about.

The market is the life-force of all Russian cities. It is here, away from the capitalistic ventures of organized retail, that ordinary Russians buy and sell their goods. Voronezh's main market was a wild crowd of people pressed into inadequate Russian fencing. It was an immense display of clothes, honey, sausages, pasta, fish, breads, milk, grains, jewelry, vegetables, cassette tapes, footwear, soap, toilet paper, locks, school supplies, videos, yarn, bras, candles, perfumes, spices, and just about anything else that can be sold from one person to another. The finalities of cattle and boar hung from hooks. There were bloodied axes ready to cut and the butchers looked like madmen in their blood covered aprons.

Marina knew the market well and guided me to products I'd need during my stay. I have simple tastes and do my grocery shopping in places where blood is not a typical part of the scenario. My experience with cooking is minimal, and although the market was great for a host of other items, I refused to buy my meat there, lacking the stomach to watch my meal get hacked from pig to pork, cow to beef.

Within the fenced area, there were hundreds of tables set up, and each set of tables was under a thin canopy that kept the rain off the merchandise. The paths between these tents were always crowded, no matter the day or time thereof. On weekends the crowds would bulge from the middle and spill onto the streets.

The venders worked on abacuses with amazing speed, which made it impossible for me to detect any overcharging.

There were times when the marketplace was the place to buy from. Soap, dishes or shoelaces were a good deal cheaper than inside the department store. And it was truly Russian. I loved nearly every bit of it. I would first stop at an old woman who sold breads, big round Armenian ones called *lavash*. She would spread a thick layer of goopy sauce onto it then I would fold these into crescents and continue about collecting things. I bought my bathtub-friendly laundry detergent and toothpaste here. I found a scarf and a t-shirt too. Many times I would help the local economy by buying all my cigarettes here. The stalls of a market are a must for any traveller who wants to feel Russia because they are always among the most vibrant, not to mention economically solid, places in town.

In response to my aversion to fresh meat carcasses, Marina took me to the Russia department store and to *Electronika*, both of which served shrink-wrapped meats that were guaranteed not to be dog or cat. Electronika was familiar; like a déjà-vu but half that. The store was a Russian attempt at the First-World. It was the only place in the city with imported magazines, imported CDs and pinball games that tilt themselves.

Much of Voronezh was no different today from what it was forty years ago. It was obliterated by the Germans in a two-year standoff during World War Two or, as it is known in Russia, the Great Patriotic War. That's a big thing here. It seems like it happened a week ago. Most of the buildings were rebuilt with Stalin's unimaginative design decisions. Others are towers of Soviet pride. When the few Soviet-designed triumphs are seen, they dominate; they are landmarks.

On the edge of the city, high over the river mist, stood the

War Memorial. An expanse of flower beds sat between a proud obelisk and the Eternal Flame. The flame rose from an iron star and was wreathed in fresh flowers. Beyond it stood an enormous patriotic statue of marching soldiers. In the depths of my mind, I knew this memorial had grounded itself and would, if I choose, let me adopt it. And it did. There were a lot of people around, drinking and looking out at the great display given by the river and the Left Bank. But they weren't there reflecting on the war. They weren't giving the obelisk its reason for being. I was. I was attentive to every detail, marveling at the memory as well as the old Soviet soldiers forged into the view.

In Canada, I took a great humbling read of our own history and our participation in the wars for freedom. Sadly, for so many the world wars are just ghosts, old stories, black and white footage played at double speed. My freedom was just given to me. In Russia a ferocity, with an incurable resentment, keeps the Eternal Flame lit. The cost of lives in the Great Patriotic War isn't a wound in Russia, it's a lost son. Germany ate through lives like a plague. When the German army overran Voronezh, they left four percent of the city standing and carried on to Stalingrad.

I explored the area around my flat, the streets and dead-ends, the trams, and trolley-busses, and I acclimatized to the spirit and appeal. Voronezh proper is situated on a bluff on the right bank.

Uptown Voronezh holds the commercial core, the city's center and the bulk of the history on main street, *Prospect Revolution*. From there, the slope to the river is steep and cluttered with tiny wooden homes guiding the severely under-maintained streets.

The Prospect was sided with businesses, offices and shops. The route housed the only movie theatre in town and the central post office. If there was anything cosmopolitan, or any shops in which to buy high-end mascara, sunglasses, or quality imports in the whole city, it was on the Prospect. One end of Prospect anchored Lenin's Square with a confident statue of Vladimir. Behind him stood the local government Duma building. Lenin looked down a few kilometres of Prospect where it joined Koltsovskaya at the train station. Plexhanovskaya, near my apartment, crossed them where they were spread about a half-kilometre apart. The main streets from my flat were Plex-hanovskaya, Prospect Revolution, and Koltsovskaya. That was the Russian triangle.

There's a distressing problem in Russia. Traffic lights and street lights frequently don't work. This is not a problem of engineering; it is because thieves steal the copper wiring from them to sell on the black market. This results in many uncontrolled intersections and dark parts of town. If bricks suddenly became valuable, Voronezh would be leveled by sunrise.

Voronezh is big. There are conflicting opinions about the population so it falls between 700,000 and one million. No two sources can agree. Voronezh was, until recently, one of 90 'closed towns' in Russia where Soviet secrecy persisted. And it was honoured as a 'Hero City' for its involvement during the war. There were special coins in circulation that depicted the ten *hero cities* of the Soviet Union.

No account of Russia would be complete without using the word 'nuclear' at least twice. Russians have always been technologically capable. Aside from sophisticated weaponry and unparalleled filing systems, they developed nuclear power plants in great numbers. Voronezh has its own haunting device. The Novovoronets Nuclear Power Plant is Russia's oldest nuclear plant with pressurized-water reactors. It is situated close to a military training field. In March of 1995, an out-of-control rocket exploded just a few kilometres from the power plant. In

July 1996 two un-detonated bombs were found in a nearby canal. Despite the external worries, the internal deserve some attention. A ten-year list of emergency shutdowns goes like this:

- December 1990: control element discovered damaged.
- October 1991: failure of shutdown system during refueling.
- March 1992: technical failure.
- March 1992: failure of automatic shutdown system.
- April 1992: breakdown of cooling system.
- July 1992: failure of cooling system.
- August 1992: failure of shutdown system.
- August 1997: leakage of radioactive water.

Voronezh was losing its summer to the late September climes and the trees were littering big proud leaves along the broken roads. Marina and I walked for long days witnessing pieces of the city she hadn't ventured to in years. The Great Patriotic War memorial, the Wedding Bridge, and the Church of the Shroud are the dominant treasures of the city. Karl Marx Street is a pedestrian route connecting two main roads and it is wide, green and filled with full trees, clustered homes, babushkas, and children chasing children. It was here that we usually strolled back to my flat in the evenings.

The two public places with access to the internet were filled—a private venture called *Informsvyaz* and the library. Both had ten computers and were inexpensive for internet usage, but they were filled, mainly with black students. Marina explained that persons from African nations came to Russia to study where higher education was both possible and affordable. Marina confided that there was a racial wall. Russians did not associate with the Africans. The result was the Africans emailing home.

Just off Lenin Square was a small bank with four chairs and a soldier with a machine gun. I thought my travellers' cheques would be readily received everywhere I wanted to be. It took many carbon forms, frequent office huddles, and the blessing of the manager to confirm that I was who I was and that the cheques were what they were. After this time-consuming first impression, I knew I would only be doing large transactions. I did a quick bow to the gentleman in the camouflage with the machine gun on my way out. He would see me again and I wanted him to remember I was nice to him.

Despite the irregularities of products and services, I liked Voronezh and its pace of life. It is a moderately attractive city to the traveller's eye if you can ignore begging limbless soldiers, stray packs of dogs, and gypsies sleeping in parks. Voronezh has a character of its own. The weather had been great. The official temperature is still controlled by the state so autumn, I was told, will be pleasing.

———————

The day arrived for me to be formally introduced to the Institute. It was with anticipation disguised as dread. Marina told me I would first have a meeting with the school president, then two hours later I would have my first class. I hurried through the shower routine and dressed in the breeze that coursed through my flat. As the minutes ticked by, I rearranged furniture and checked the gas situation again. My biggest fear was to leave the apartment, only to look back and see a fiery cloud erupt because the small valve hadn't completely squeezed off the gas.

At the appointed time, I left the apartment saying a far-ranging prayer covering everything from the presidents' meeting to irreparable damage to my home. I closed the door and turned all three locks. It was a dark flight of stairs down to the door and then I was into sunshine. It was exactly 777 steps from my flat to the Institute.

I reached my place of work. There were two sets of doors side by side and another identical set inside. One overwhelmingly Russian trait is to unlock adjacent doors and not put up notices reading 'This Door Is Locked'. This is perhaps sensible since the peculiar habit, I was told, was to minimize the drafts that wreak havoc on the heating systems. That I understood. But the next day different doors will be locked, as they do not like using the same configuration every day. That I did not understand.

There was a maze of students on the front steps and all had to look me over before returning to their cigarettes. I had a proud smile to offer them. Then I chose the wrong set of doors. One door in four was unlocked. I tried three with my scholarly grin and noticed half-smiles in response. This same scene played out on the inside set of doors.

An old woman was selling homemade cakes, breads and cookies on a small wooden table in the small foyer. Next to her was a security booth with armed guards, dressed in fatigues. I knew where I was going, so I slipped by with a quick wave and paced on to the second floor without being stopped. The guards, though, were busy searching through the knapsack of a student who looked far less suspicious than I felt I looked. And they were putting on the rubber gloves for him.

After stumbling upon the accounting department, computer lab, and two classrooms in session, I found the foreign language office. Marina was there, superbly dressed. Her hair was short, almost boyish, and copper-coloured because a shipment of copper dye had come to the market.

'And how are we this morning, Mr. Antonson?' she smiled and patted my shoulder.

'My respect for flame has grown exponentially,' I said.

'Oh come on. Did you follow the checklist?' she asked.

'I bet you go through foreigners like soap... hey, what is with the doors? Is there an order to which ones are unlocked? Does a committee meet every morning to decide which doors they'll use? I just want into the building, not Mensa,' I asked. Marina explained the drafts and the mitigating role of the doors. She also said that it was standard practice in Russia. I decided to drop the issue and focus on the meeting. Marina checked her watch and offered me a tea. Sasha walked in with a bunch of clipped papers snug under his arm.

'Well Brant, how are you today? All ready to meet the president?' He smiled and shook my hand.

'I am as ready as I'll ever be. Actually, tomorrow would be better.' I said.

Marina set down the tea and placed two sugar cubes beside a small creamer. Teas from all over the world are brought to Russia, and Russians demand only the best. Russians love tea like Americans love coffee. I would not enjoy one decent cup of coffee in Russia. If there was coffee, it was instant. And while I like instant coffee, the Russian instant coffee was not good. It goes straight to the nerves and colon. But Russian tea, or more accurately *chai*, is the most popular drink after vodka, wine, and beer. Where alcohol wasn't present, there was chai.

The president's secretary called. It was time for me to make an impression. The caffeine from the tea went straight to my nerves and colon. I followed Marina down the hall. The Institute was undergoing the biggest renovations the building had ever seen. There were workmen drilling, cutting and fixing parts of the hallway.

I stepped inside the President's office and greeted the secretary and all of the other people waiting to see someone. Marina shared a few words with the secretary who in turn phoned the president. I regretted the tea, the cubes of sugar and the cream, and I wondered if my apartment was burning.

The president was a medium-sized man with dark hair and a firm handshake. His full name was Yuli Zolotovinski, though he said Yuli would be fine. It seemed absurd I should call him by his first name, for he was the brass of this facility that had lured me far from home, but I'd already forgotten his last name. Yuli invited us into his office and encouraged us to sit. The room was decorated with paintings and trinkets he'd acquired within Russia and abroad. Marina translated and though I felt the urge to reply when I understood a line or a word in Russian, I did not. Marina was thoroughly competent as a translator for she seldom was caught without an English variant of the intense speech Yuli was issuing. Yuli wrung his hands and spoke with pride of the school's history, the number of satellite schools in the surrounding area, and the remarkable improvements to the building itself.

Voronezh has a sister city—Farmville, Virginia. Yuli commented that it had been his good fortune to visit America. Canada, however, was untapped. He spoke of building relationships with Canadian schools and forging joint academic programs. I was, it seemed, an ambassador for Canada and what I thought, said or did would reflect my country's perspective. I praised Canada and I praised Russia but I did not praise America. Yuli had a small but prominent American flag on a shelf. I would, in a day's time, present him with a Canadian flag twice its size. And Yuli would put the flags together. I had little against America, but I was well aware that I would be thought of as American while I stayed there. I had to maintain my identity. I had to fight not to be American and then fight to be Canadian, not British, Australian or a New Zealander. It had been my hope from the start that I would be able to become as Russian as I could. But most people would presume me to be American.

Yuli, though, did not think of me as American, quite the opposite. In fact *he* above all people knew I was Canadian and wanted from me that which was Canadian. Yuli articulated that we could build bridges between our countries. I was fully prepared to do my part if I had a part to play. I wasn't in any echelon that permitted me to build super-sized contacts but I told Yuli that he had me and my support and that both were as Canadian as could be. I told him I was honoured to be under his leadership and a part of his school. And I added that I would do whatever I could to help whenever possible (for some reason I put my hands up in the air at right angles) with the building of bridges. Marina translated a few closing words and with that we were done....

There were three computers in the foreign language office. Sasha had one, Elena the secretary had another, and the third was for the use of whichever teacher got to it first. It was from this old computer that I could freely email home. I didn't feel comfortable in the office environment. The room was small and the computers were very close together. There was little space to collect thoughts and email them home, especially with curious Russians behind me. So I rarely ever used the third computer. I preferred, despite the added expense, to use my laptop in the surroundings of my flat. There, I had access to chai, food, and cigarettes.

A young woman with tossed-salad hair and glasses came in and leapt on the third computer. Marina had been marking assignments and put her pen down. She said a few Russian words and then introduced me to Lucia. Lucia was from Italy and was teaching Italian. She spoke Italian, Russian, and French. I took French for six long years in an immersion program at school. All throughout my twenties, though, I seldom had the chance to speak it. When I met Lucia, I stumbled out words that I'd not used in fifteen years. Lucia was a bit rusty, having also taken hers years before. The language bridged something between us. And as I gained confidence in my French, the Russians around us became suspicious. No one else could understand us and speaking French became the clue that we were talking about the assembly design data of tanks.

Marina checked her watch at the same moment the bell rang. It was time for my first class. I followed Marina's lead up the staircase to the third floor. Students were spilling from rooms and checking the computer print-outs stapled to the wall for their next classes.

Marina locked her index finger on the day of the week then ran it across to the time. I was teaching in Room 305.

I opened the door to find five students looking at me. Four young women and a young man sat at two of the eight long tables. Marina entered first and clasped her hands together.

'All right class, the moment you have been waiting for is here. This is Mr. Antonson and he will be your new English teacher. I am sure you'll treat him with courtesy and respect. Welcome to your first class Mr. Antonson,' said Marina, '*Oodachi*… or Good luck.'

With that Marina left. I made my way to the front and put my pack on the table. I had anticipated, and predicted this moment, though I had not entirely prepared for it. The bell rang and the class began. Instinctively I picked up a heavy, square piece of chalk and wrote my name out in full. I introduced myself and told them I preferred my first name be used when addressing me. I counted them. There were still only the five students, all in their early twenties. It occurred to me that although I'd been told they were third-year students, they might not be that expressive or fluent in English. So I started with a slow introduction. I explained briefly who I was and where I came from. I had purchased a map of Canada from the Queen's printer and I tried to secure it to the wall. A young man spoke up and introduced himself as Slava. His English was quite good and he said he would go and retrieve tape for the map. In his absence I smiled at the four women. Each in sequence was beautiful, pretty, cute and attractive. Slava returned with thumbtacks. I could smell cigarette smoke. On this particular map, Canada was shown as though it were taken from a globe. This meant that Moscow sat on the edge of the horizon, the upper right hand corner. It gave a grand perspective of the relative distance I'd travelled to be there. I felt a little strange looking at it there on the wall. I had come halfway around the world to be right where I was standing, in front of my very first class.

I turned to the students. Who were they and where were they from? Slava was aggressive and impatient. These qualities would personify him the whole year. He lived on the Left Bank, in an apartment where they shared a phone line with the neighbours. He was from Petrozavosk near the Arctic Circle and had nearly stayed there and become a train engineer. He was reading his third Somerset Maugham novel and his goal was to visit America, particularly Chicago and New York. His favorite movies… but I stopped him. Slava would have eagerly run out the clock, and while I appreciated this attribute, I felt confident the women could do that too. I could always go back to him.

Nina had been born and raised in the Ukraine. She was tall, with short dark hair and a fresh face. Her family had moved to Voronezh when her army father was transferred.

Nona was a striking girl with a round face, almost pudgy, in an attractive way, and long blond hair. She was from Kazakhstan and had, along with her army father, lived in Germany and other cities in Russia. Her English was minimal and though

I tried to coax the words from her, she just stared at a spot on the ceiling thinking in Russian or German or Kazakh.

Olya, perhaps the spotlight of the school, was radiant. Her hair changed shades in the light. Her clothes were expensive and her voice shushed the room. For all her beauty and jewelry, she displayed a simple and unflattering attitude. 'I was born in Voronezh, I live in Voronezh, and I will die in Voronezh,' she said without cracking what I knew was a beautiful smile. School and formal conversing were weak points in her character. Slava confided to me later that since she fell in love with Boris, she'd lost all hope for education and others. Boris must be quite the machine, I thought. To turn her mind away from her potential, clearly, there were good men to be found in Russia.

Anya was blonde and decorated with a few amber items. She was pretty yet robust. Her hands were tough and worn and she looked exhausted and probably always would. Anya lived in a small town called Grafskaya and each day she awoke at five to milk her cows. I'd never met anyone who actually used a yoke. Then she would take a train to school. She was living a truly Russian life. I had a weakness for her.

For all of the students, I learned education was their job. This was post-secondary schooling and their studies kept them from being in the workforce, or in Slava's case, the army. They had to love English and with coaxing, even the withdrawn contributed.

My first class was small and it was with them that I became closest. The next day I would meet other classes with many second and fourth year students in them. And I would struggle with their names and get to know only pieces of them. But the third years, Slava, Nina, Olya, Nona, and Anya would be my jewels. I could focus better on the limited class. They quickly adjusted to me and I embraced them as friends.

Days on, it was Russian National Teacher's Day. I was receptive to any holiday that weighed in my favour. The students brought me homemade cookies and asked to go to the park. I obliged because the last few classes had been rather quiet. I had done most of the talking with Slava a close second. There wasn't a third place. The third-year girls were shy and non-vocal. This is not what a first-time teacher wants. There is supposed to be active participation, the thrusting of arms in the air and cries of 'Me, me, pick me! Oh my God I know this one!' There should be willing contributions and partaking in the glorious language that is English. I agreed to the park idea because, firstly, I wanted to see them outside their classroom demeanors and secondly, they said this was permitted. (Marina would later look at me with a wince that I would learn to fear and tell me it was not permitted.)

All it took was a lungful of fresh air and they completely opened up. The shyness of our first few classes evaporated as we talked and walked among the golden leaves of early autumn. They fell from the trees in cyclical fashion and rolled across the streets. We found benches and started our class. A famous fountain, reputed to have been long-dead, sputtered alive and the focus of the class changed. The fountain owned the attention of passers-by too. Time unwound and we headed back to the school to split off to our respective next classes.

I lingered until the day's final class because I'd been told there was to be a welcoming party and I was the guest of honour. In the office, the staff came in one by one and greeted me with hugs and chocolate. Lucia was also new and she'd been given a welcome a month earlier. It began there in the office, that night; Lucia and I grew fond of one another. It was there we spoke French and it was there we got our first suspicious looks.

The other teachers who taught English met me in the office.

Tatyana was a wonderful woman, older in years. She was haggard and her teaching career spanned many decades, many students and many schools. I was a welcome sight to her. She entrusted me with her valued third years. My presence also helped another teacher, Olga. She was running between classes too. I had a schedule of regular classes and, as Tatyana or Olga needed, additional covering classes. There was a chill in my body when I heard these 'English' teachers speak English. They had thick Russian accents and I concluded it is no wonder all Russians sound the same when they speak English, their *teachers* had poor accents. It is perpetuated from teacher to student. But the chill came from realizing that I, as a mother tongue English speaker, was a valued asset.

Ten of us sat around while some sang Russian songs and others made a meal out of bread, cucumber, and tomatoes. When the vodka was cracked open, arms were raised in high toasts to God, the Motherland and to, of course, the new recruit. I was asked to listen to Georgian songs and drink Georgian wine. Sasha, wearing the suit I never much liked, sang the bass for an amazing assortment of music. They pushed me to sing and I told them to line up five shooters. I sang parts of three Billy Joel songs and ended with a little Cowboy Junkies.

I asked if they would humour me and sing the anthem, the one from Soviet days (there were, at the time, no words for the anthem. The Soviet version was the last with lyrics). Not only did they humour me but they all stood and goose-stepped as they had when they were younger. It was a Communist conga line. The Soviet Pioneers were the national group of young people. Several of my colleagues had been Pioneers and for them this brought back many memories, some happy, some sad.

Cigarettes were lit in the office, a punishable offence during the day. We sat on the desks, downloaded music onto work computers and faxed our buttocks to other departments. Vodkainduced smiles turned to song; laughs turned to dancing. I was mesmerized. There I was in the arms of the faculty looking at my peers from an altogether fresh view. It was during this party I signed my contract to work until my visa expired in January. I signed the piece of paper committing me to Russia. Moments don't come much finer.

I found my apartment. Vodka and I are demonically opposed. The third and sixth reasons are that I tend to wander. Even though my friends walked me home and came in for tea, I left soon after they did. I wore my hat in the night. Not just any hat but a fedora, the hat that says I live life in italics. I brought it along expecting a few months of favourable wearing conditions. I took out the pipe my father had given me. I liked smoking it although a 31 year old pipe smoker is rare - and it is complicated with its various gadgets and the fussing, stuffing, and tamping. Marina said I looked serious with a pipe and that cigarettes made me look like just another smoker. I pinched tobacco into my pipe and stumbled along coughing. The sky stopped just above the city. I paused beside an old Russian apartment building at the end of my street where it met a rail yard. I scanned the windows and contemplated the lives that were being lived in the shadows behind them. I mused jovially about the night and the sincere welcome I had been given. For someone who'd been prepared for a minimum of comfort, I felt I had been bestowed with knighthood. The stars spun in the night and dusty Ladas zipped by without any notice of me. I'd seen enough for one day, and I still had to make my way back.

Anya, the third-year class's farm girl, had pled a time or two for me to escort her to a nightclub. I persistently refused on the grounds that I was ten years older than the demographic and I was her teacher. I didn't need to see a nightclub. She persisted and I gave in on the condition that it was nothing close to a relationship-bound night. I certainly wasn't about to start a relationship with a student. I feared that, at a nightclub, I'd be seen with Anya and my year away would begin to end immediately following that. She promised, in her limited English, that this was as friends.

On a breezy Friday evening, I met Anya outside a storefront on Karl Marx Street. I began to chit-chat with her and soon found her English to be locked up inside her mouth. She made valiant attempts at conversation, but we would always end with our chins up gazing at the setting sun. I felt awkward. The nightclub didn't open until nine and we'd met at seven. This left some serious silence. I tried my Russian and with her encouragement, formulated whole phrases. Anya spoke in Russian; English was forgotten for the night. Somehow we had many conversations. I gathered from her charades that there was a 'whole lotta farm' in this small town girl. I looked at my watch. It was seven-thirty.

A quarreling, multi-coloured light show fronted the 'Flamingo'. We checked our coats and I was accosted for our cover charges. Without her buoyant winter coat Anya was stupendous, with her Russian hourglass figure intact. She knew she looked daring in her dress. It pressed her breasts together like gears. The evening was daring enough, I thought. We walked up a staircase to a warehouse room full of intoxicated teenagers. Lights strobed about the walls and spat silhouettes across the dance floor. We each ordered a Sprite from the bar and moved to a corner. There was barely room to walk and bodies brushed against bodies. A huge projection screen was showing Swiss models on a catwalk via an intermittent satellite connection. The club killed any hopes of romance.

I ordered two more Sprites and occasionally glanced at Anya. She looked perturbed. I suppose she thought I'd dance, but I didn't. Maybe she thought they'd play a few slow songs, but they didn't. Maybe she thought we'd have fun, but we didn't. After two hours, we left. Arm in arm, we walked back to my flat. I thought she'd come in for a moment, no more. She felt obliged to. I knew she lived a great distance outside of town and I grappled with the thought that it was 'just' late enough that she was stuck in the city. I knew her best friend and classmate Nona was a solution though I wasn't sure that those were her intentions.

She spent the night.

Nona never answered her phone so Anya and I sat around my flat discussing strategies. At four a.m. I bade her goodnight, left a small kiss on her forehead and tossed her a blanket so she could organize herself on the couch. I was treading water and fearful that the event would be discussed to a sickening degree if it got out. I should say, though, that Anya was the sort of woman I could attach myself to. She was preciously naïve, built strong and sturdy in a traditional 'Russian' way. She was 22 years old and maturing every day. I instinctively knew she wanted to be mine. It had been apparent through most school classes by her winking and the carving of my name into her binders. There were no girlfriend/boyfriend relationships; Anya was going for the golden ring of marriage. I figured all this out in the bathroom.

In class one day, the third years told me they were going to cook me dinner. On a Sunday afternoon Anya, Nina, Olya, Nona and Slava showed up at my flat and the women took over the kitchen. Slava and I surfed the internet. Lucia, who taught the same students Italian, came to make authentic spaghetti. My flat was small and my kitchen was not meant to hold five women at the same time. Somehow, in Russian tradition, the girls slaved for hours and fit like a puzzle. They laughed and cleaned and kneaded things. Lucia swore at length in Italian as the Russian pasta and sub-standard ingredients for the sauce sent her over the edge.

Since its release, I'd had a craving to watch the movie *'Gone In Sixty Seconds'*. Clearly, by the trailer, with its swerving cars and jamming gears, I was destined to see this amazing film. I found out that the Russian version, edited with a Russian voice-over and Arabic sub-titles, was available at every video kiosk. The problem was finding a VCR. It was during this time that I asked Slava about watching the movie. I thought we could rent a VCR and proposed that to him. He said renting something was absurd. I said his attitude was absurd.

'We borrow or we take… we do not rent,' he said.

I said to him that VCRs could be rented the world 'round. At my request, we stalked the city and I discovered conclusively that my idea was completely wrong. You can't even rent a car in Voronezh. Slava said a company used to rent cars but nobody brought them back. The concept seemed as foreign as I was. Not having access to video machines doubtlessly left a number of video illiterates.

So I bought a paper and Slava found a classified ad for a used VCR. It was asking 700 rubles or about $35 US dollars. Slava called while Lucia was hollering at the students in Italian. Slava confirmed the sale was still open. We could, Anya said, just hop on a tram and get it. Anya, who had the least to do with the dinner preparations, agreed to come as I had little confidence I could get there alone. It was off my map. Slava had held out for time on my computer then decided to come at the last minute to make sure I wasn't taken advantage of.

When a Russian says 'It's not far', it means anything under a day. Boarding a tram, we carried on for an agonizingly cold and loud hour. Russians are typically people of endurance and this didn't phase anyone but me. The cost of a tram is two rubles but the tram tickets say 30 kopecks (100 kopecks = one ruble. 33 rubles = 1 US dollar). There is no money to replace the old tickets of which, I guessed, there was still a warehouse full. We ended up in the outskirts of nowhere, climbed four dark storeys and entered a small, flamboyantly wallpapered flat. The VCR was the first Soviet model ever made. It was from 1971, weighed 25 pounds and came with six spare belts of varying sizes. I got it for twenty dollars.

The long tram ride back from the city's edge was at dusk, far later than I had planned. We eventually sat down in my dark living room and pressed 'play'. The video system was PAL/Secam which basically means it is black and white with orange highlights and the screen was formatted so it looks as if you are watching it through a fish bowl. The English was quite low but the single translator (who did the entire film (every character) in his monotone, devoid of the car-chasing vocal elements) was three times louder in Russian. The Arabic subtitles blocked the bottom third of the screen. It was a disappointment, the movie included. But I could say I owned a Russian VCR and due to the bulky area it took up, it was often a good conversation piece.

As my first month in Russia concluded and the clocks went back an hour to accommodate a solstice, I started a list of protocols I'd learned in my first thirty days:

- Holding open a door for anyone is an act of cowardice.
- Do not smile in public unless you are under six or too drunk to remember where you have to wake up.
- There will be nights when you will wear a scarf to bed.

- A 12-letter word that starts with 'TSCH' means 'Don't think of passing beyond this gate because the dog won't bark before disfiguring you'.
- There are two types of drivers... those who honk and those whose horns don't work.
- I live 20 kilometers from hunter-gatherers.
- Anything can be made to work if you fiddle with it long enough.
- I can check my 'room temperature' on www.weather.com.
- Most of the traditional fur hats are dog fur.
- The word 'communism' isn't used in conversation as often as you'd think.
- If you trip over rubble, shaking your fist at it clears you from blame.
- Everything in Russia doubles as a bottle opener.
- Plugging in a 110v device into a 220v socket ruins the device and the socket.
- Never knock on a car window and ask the four men why they've been sitting there for six hours.
- If nobody uses it, there's a reason.
- Hammer-and-sickle in Russian is '*Serp i Molot*'
- If you order 200g of cheese, they make one guess, one decisive cut, weigh it, and you pay.
- If the wooden fire escape burns, there's always the concrete stairs inside the building.
- A lot of people will run if you chase them.

Sasha approached me one afternoon after class with a new contract. He asked if I'd like an extension, to work the year out. The Institute was happy with my progress so far.

I agreed immediately.

I liked Voronezh, I liked the people I associated with and I was in no hurry to return to Canada. When the contract was laid out, I scanned over the Russian agreement and signed my name to the line below it. It was here that I first saw my name was transliterated 'Brant'. In the Romanized translation from Cyrillic, *Brant* was more appropriate than the short 'e' *Brent* which is pronounced 'ye' and led to butchering when attempted. When I was in Estonia, no one called me anything but *Brant* and at the time it irritated me. Actually Estonia irritated me. Come to think of it, the world was a pretty bad place at that time. But as I looked at 'Brant' sitting there, I decided to change my name. I would pen all future works under the name *Brant Antonson*. It would be my coming of age. I no longer wanted to change my name to Samuel Clemens. I notified everyone at home that I was changing my name to Brant. I outlined the reasons and stopped short of changing my middle name to Zhivago. It would be so easy to remember. I loved the gentle *Brantushka* the other teachers addressed me by and Anya liked to call me by my full name all run together as *Bran'anonson*. Lucia, offering an Italian spin, always called me *Brantutso*. But Brant was so perfect that I accepted it as fate.

I never bought chicken from the 'chicken kiosk' because Marina said they have blood in the spines. Instead, I would buy a few *caseeskas*, hotdogs in pastry, everyday for seven cents. The faculty wanted to tell me the ingredients however I told them I'd quit and go to an enemy institute to teach. I was fully into caseeskas. Sometimes on the way to work and always on the way home. I would watch the woman under her little canopy make every one. She cooked them in fours on a little griddle. She would fire a small stick into one hotdog after another and lay them down on the grill, then cover them with a doughy mixture. After two or three minutes, they would be golden brown. I then had my choice of the spicy-*garchitsa* sauce, mustard or ketchup. I had two or three of these a day with alternating sauces. They were cheap by comparison to a lunch, and quick. I had no idea that I would develop an intolerance to them. However, after a few weeks I had a physiological aversion to them and, sadly, I would just pass the stand and the old woman with a knowing smile. She seemed to understand.

I was alternating days between the second and third year classes. There were upwards of 20 students in the second year. They were noticeably weaker in their vocabulary, structure, and abilities to express. There was a lot more confidence per student in the larger classes and they fought to answer my questions. There was soon an even bigger difference in numbers between the two classes. Olya was in a bad car accident and was therefore absent. Boris, it seemed, had a drinking problem and in his denial had driven himself and my student into a power pole. The car was split in half and sadly only Boris came out unscathed. It was my first experience feeling such anxiety for a student. Olya would be in the hospital for three months and refused all visitors. This left me with four students in the third year. Between the groups, I was settling into the schedule, anticipating bells and meeting my lessons prepared and eager. I learned how to be the architect of time, how to construct a class and have it spent wisely.

I made up a list of idioms, expressions, words that few Russians knew. This list developed into five pages. The chalkboards were horrific. The chalk, when there was any, was prone to shattering and slivers. The brushes were only brushes by name so as to distinguish them from chalk or an electrical outlet. I would mark off words on the board and see how many students knew the difference between 'catching a bus' and 'catching the flu' or 'catching a busflu'. This merriment went on through several classes with each student dutifully copying down my explanations and phrases where one might find the words in use. There were classes where even Tatyana or Olga, the teachers, would sit in and take notes.

One type of teaching wizardry I used was music. From my wide collection of compact disks, I would pull a choice and copy the lyrics onto my computer. Then I would remove particular words or whole lines of song depending on the level of the audience. Van Halen, Tim McGraw, and Billy Joel were popular. The greatest challenge of all this lesson work, providing I could have it printed, was finding power. I would bring my portable disk player to class along with small and 'just-loud-enough' speakers. As the institute was being remodeled, each class was held in a different and unfamiliar room. It became apparent that the new theme was to leave each room with one power outlet and that it be located no lower than seven feet high. We used, at times, massive coils of 220V extension cord to get music from my small disk player. And, if I was lucky, the exercise and preparation would take at least half of the class time.

The rest of the time I worked out of a photocopied study book from England's Headway program the students had been using. There were days when Tatyana would shake things up and ask if I would work the classes through the past-perfect, detail contractions, or lecture on non-Euclidean grammar. My interest in languages helped me endure what would have been a savage and cruel thing were I not fascinated in the product. I learned the night before or quite literally in class, just what the class was learning. One night a student dropped by my apartment. Nastya rang my bell and asked if I could 'check her passive voice'. And so, I learned the passive voice.

It is a funny thing that we use our language skills without the honour, respect and courtesy they deserve. It is strange that a social drop-out can beg on a Canadian street using a free range of participles, tenses, and declensions, asking for spare change without pride in it all. In Russia, the students were engaged in my classes and getting quicker and sharper daily; they wanted, needed, and were striving for the careless way English speakers speak. The way native English speakers interact with everything in everyday life is taken for granted. From choosing movies to reading road signs, English governs our every moment. In Russia, our language is the golden ring.

I was surrounded by Russian. If I wanted to run down and grab a drink, buy bread, or I happen to run into the school's president at the urinals, I *had to* communicate in Russian. I was such an oddity in Voronezh that old people stopped me and asked to see proof I was from Canada. They are old Soviets and hadn't seen a foreigner since the Germans in '45. Everything around me was in Russian; everything was in an alphabet that is exciting and enigmatic. The Russian alphabet consists of 33 letters: 21 consonants, 10 vowels, and two letters without sound. **Я случайно установил ненужную панель инструментов и теперь не могу ее убрать. Вот в чем фигня** means 'I accidentally installed an unwanted toolbar and now I can't remove it. That's the shits.'

The students wanted my language, my dialect, my collo-quial speech, and every time I wrote something on the board, they had to recognize it and absorb it if they wanted to surf websites, watch a Hollywood blockbuster without mismatched lips, or become an air traffic controller. English is where the world's at; to them it was essential. And to attain fluency is their dream.

As I learned Russian, I climbed into a language whose words are out of familiar order, which had new stresses and syntax and modifications for gender that were beyond me. I realized the challenges in the minds of my students. As they learned from me, I learned from them.

When I was living in Estonia, I watched Russian signs come down as independence took hold. Estonian was in Roman script and the language didn't have much future as it was very difficult and spoken by a small segment of the world's population. But Russian contained an enchanting potential, a secret door. After four years of self-study, night courses, and a trip across Siberia, I still had to work it; I needed to use Russian to live.

I could no longer see English as a regular Canadian does. My daily thoughts were no longer simple tasks. If I wasn't teaching English structure, I was speaking in French with Lucia or trying out my Russian on people. I couldn't speak to anyone in plain ole' everyday English. I had to see myself as the only person in Voronezh who knew why a British accent can sound pompous or educated, what Bugs Bunny really means when he says 'Nya, what's up, doc', and who could tell a Bronx accent from a Mississippi one.

I thought about the typical Canadian city buzzing about. The supermarket, bookstores, the notary public, a drive-thru; how easy it all is. The fleeting simplicity in watching a movie, reinstalling an operating system, reading a book or asking for an empty cup because the first is hot enough to web your fingers, is truly a gift. Our mouths and tongues move in a manner that leaves little misunderstood. We can fully appreciate the Simpsons, the power in our advertising, and read Shakespeare as Shakespeare wrote it. I thought about Chinese and East Indians, Vietnamese, and other recent immigrants to Vancouver, trying like my students and myself, to grapple with characters, sounds, and contexts never seen before. And at the same time, trying to accept a new city, culture, and criminal code as home. At last, I could empathize.

I had brought along several pieces of luggage, though normally I wouldn't have, since I had already learned that weight is a travellers' foe. Carrying excessive clothes, toiletries, and anything with a pneumatic nozzle is always a severe draw-back to mobility. But on this trip, where I was planning on actu-ally living, working, and playing, I had packed four pieces of luggage with as much as they could hold. I had suits and ties, sweaters, and long underwear. I also had books. Books for me and books for students. Books on the Soviet Union and books on travelling in Poland. Philosophy, the sciences, and a handful of magazines. I had, to my amazement, brought enough books to fill the entire bookshelf at my flat. For some reason, in my methodical packing, these had all been on my short-list. You never know when you are going to need inset A4-Cheyenne in an American road atlas, a Dummies guide to DOS, or be called upon to explain to someone how you can collapse a wave-func-tion just by watching.

In preparation for teaching abroad, I had searched my home city for books on teaching English. Even as I left, I was not confident I would be able to pull off a year teaching. I only had a superficial teaching degree and the rest was bridled fear and not confidence (my training seemed to involve a lot of singing). There were stores and teachers' outlets where I was able to pick up training manuals, alphabet tracers, and posters of the 'A is for Apple' sort.

I didn't even know prior to arriving what level of profi-ciency the students would have. Sasha had emailed me that they were second and third year English classes. To me that meant they were adults though they had the English language skills of children in the second or third grade. It really meant that they had had six years of English in High School and were in their second and third years at a graduate level. Still, while searching for material, I did not know this nor would it have made much difference. Teaching was going to be a considerable challenge however it unfolded.

The teaching stores I visited had two variations of material:

simple or dry. The simplistic was high on substance but low on sophistication. The dry was quite dry. It was literature that had little to offer me in the short time I had to prepare. Many were novel length books that covered every facet of engineering a class or designer plans for making the most out of an hour with cooperative students. I mostly gathered books and material in the 'simple' genre. Although most had pictures and used big letters, I felt happier that I could wade through them myself. There were essential books for teachers that had class plans, structured class outlines, and basic tenets of how to drag out the time allotted. I spent a fortune on these and other items that, since I was now a teacher, caught my eye. I added things with the alphabet on them, from posters to placemats, rulers to binder inserts. And I had sets of alphabet fridge magnets for reasons unknown.

I also bought (and this was foresight from having been to Russia before) exercise books. Good, old-fashioned Canadian school books. Russians use graph paper to work on. As most of North America is familiar with, we use lined paper throughout school. This is unheard of in Russia. Every exercise I had returned was on a small sheet of graph paper from stapled exercise books. Every time I saw it, I wanted to draw a stop sign. I dealt out a lined paper book to each student and received hesitant looks in return when they flipped it open. I told them it looked as strange to them as graph paper did to me.

Adjacent to Lenin's Square was the small bank where Marina helped me conduct my first transaction. I soon felt confident enough to try it on my own. The transaction should be simple. With my limited Russian, my credit card would speak the rest. I waited next to the guard with the semi-automatic and scratched my face with my card. When my turn came, I faced the same nervous woman with the bad hair. She looked up and shrieked. Then she fled flailing her arms and the man with the gun moved beside me.

People were shuffling files and a fat man with a handful of papers came and stood behind me. I was a little worried. I hadn't tried to rob her. Nor would I with the security guard, his weaponry, and months of waiting for someone to shoot. So what could the problem be?

The chaos soon died down with an 'Ah-hah!'

The reason for the excitement was soon apparent. I had neglected to sign two travellers' cheques the week before. At first I figured the whole scenario was way out of hand, it'd only been $100 worth of cheques. But I realized, as the woman with the bad hair wiped her brow, the bank couldn't bear the deficit of the 3000 rubles. For all I know, I may have been responsible for her bad hair. Everyone at the bank smiled at me as though I'd saved the day.

The credit card procedure then began and took far too long. Even if the timid woman worked as fast as she could, which would contravene Russian business rules, the procedure would take nearly a half hour. First, there were many carbons involved. There was identification to be written down on two sheets of paper. There were a few minutes where the woman pulled out different files, only to glance at them and return them to their slot. Then there was five minutes where the timid woman left and did god-knows-what and, upon her return, consulted the woman in the wicket beside her for further instruction. The other woman presumably said 'Did you take his identification? Did you mark it on two sheets of paper? Did you go and do god-knows-what for five minutes?'

The first woman most certainly answered, 'Of course, then I came to get you.'

This happened with every transaction and it is only because

of the armed guard that people maintain their calm. The timid woman, hands nervously feeling around for the next task, pulled some carbons and made triplicates of a receipt. She picked up her abacus and determined it was not going to help. After all of this, the credit card was carefully swiped through an ancient card reader. I could hear the modem spool up and dial.

Anya had invited me out to her village and the only way to get there, after missing the 'morning' bus, was to take the stuffy, stinky, stand-all-the-way train. After that, it was a seven kilometer walk to her house. There were cows all over the roadways; chickens fluttered and old people leaned on their fences. Anya's family car was stolen two days before. A beat-up little Lada that was an essential part of the whole family's life was swiped. The bastards....

Anya wakes up at five every morning to milk cows for her grandparents, then goes to school in the big city of Voronezh. She has to walk to her home from that little platform. Anya knows a shortcut though, if it deserves such a title, a five kilometer march across countless fields of dull countryside. For most of the year, she walks it in the dark.

Nona made the trek with me so I wouldn't lose my way and I would fulfill my promise. We had left Voronezh by rail and then walked the distance to Anya's house. It was a small place, nothing special, and it had a loud dog to announce our arrival. Anya ran out and gave me a hug. She had waited at the train platform for three hours then given up. The two women were actually talking about this seven kilometer walk as though it were a few streets. 'Were her grandparents home?' asked Nona in simple Russian. *Nyet*, I could see Anya mouth, she had bribed them for time to host a meal for me.

Inside there were four pots on the stove, which Anya ran to

attend. I did notice that although Anya had supposedly given up on Nona and me arriving, she had cooked a meal for twenty people. This, she said, was so she could bring me the lunch I'd missed. Anya and Nona sat down in uncomfortable chairs and began talking like teenage girls. Their Russian was far too quick for me to understand much but I listened and sipped my pulpy juice with third-world ice cubes.

The pots came to a boil and both girls leapt to calm them. *Pelmenye*, Russian dumplings, was Anya's specialty and would be served a lot during the coming months. As she neatly laid out the meal, there was soup, a silver ladle, and fresh vegetables. Then there were puny potatoes and a sauce with a hint of sherry. Anya and Nona were proud of their accomplishment, everything hot and ready at the same time. And they did the whole thing without a microwave.

Following the meal, I left for a cigarette and had three. Beside Anya's was a small school that had seen better days, better generations. It was brick and aged into the ground where it sat. Of more interest was a lonely statue of Lenin in the forefront. Anya had told me that she lived beside Lenin and I had never understood what she meant. But here was Lenin, though a rather tinny and unflattering rendition of the man. I finished my cigarettes and made a truce with the dog before returning inside.

We spent the afternoon going through photo albums. This was not what I had in mind for the afternoon but I smiled, sometimes with sincerity, when I learned that whoever was in the picture was now dead. After the fifth album we got on our coats and Anya showed us around her small town. She had confided to me earlier in the month that her mother was a prostitute and her father a drunk who lived in the same village as she. Anya had seen neither for a year or two. I looked suspiciously at each and every person we passed. She told me then she was considered an orphan by the government and her tuition was paid for as a result of her absent parents.

In time, we happened upon the village cemetery which served as a shortcut to the bus stop. The graves were withered and aged with mildew and the headstones were chipped. Many had Russian Orthodox crosses, icons, or pictures of the deceased. It was a lonely place to spend eternity. Here, in a village so far from anywhere, the trees sent their knarled roots into the gated plots and wrapped their limbs together. It was eerie, though calming. Spooky, yet consoling. Anya showed us where her relatives had been laid to rest. Her uncle had been shot to death and a second cousin had succumbed to something neither Anya nor Nona could translate but they said it in Russian with gritted teeth.

The bus stop was on the main road through town. There were twelve people waiting for the bus to Voronezh. Across from the stop was a man with pieces of beef piled high on the hood of his bluish Lada. As we waited, cows spilled from a path. Soon the entire highway was filled with cattle. They were on their way home from grazing. Anya explained that each house in the village that has cows pays a cowboy to take their cattle during the day. They go out to a field and graze. The cowboy, who now rounded the path on a horse, was nudging the last of the cows out. He didn't look like an American cowboy, rather like a typical Russian male, only on a horse. He carried no lasso, he wore no hat. The bovines carried on by us, each seemingly aware of where it was going. From the hundred or so that were all around us, Anya was able to pick out the two that were hers. They were 'Simony' and 'Jolanda,' she laughed and pointed. The cows, as cows tend to in social settings, pretended not to notice her.

Back in 1994 I had arrived at Frankfurt's airport in cowboy boots. I had a hundred dollars to my name. I sought solace from a relationship that had ended after a dream-life in Wyoming failed. I was running from the world and hid myself in Estonia figuring that'd be the last place it would look. This was the acclimatizing to the former Soviet Union. All of the culture shocks happened in Tallinn. Notably, there was a reverse shock to the Estonian/Russian people I dealt with. I lived in the suburbs and going anywhere required trolleybuses. I would stand among those awaiting a trip to town. I wore suede cowboy boots, stonewash button-fly Levis, a winter coat with neon colours never before seen in the East Bloc, and I had a bright yellow Sony Walkman with yellow cords that went to my pink ears beneath a red Budweiser cap. I would turn and see the grey Estonian people with their little grey kids in grey coats under a grey sky waiting for a grey bus. Here, too, in Graf-skaya, I stood apart from the other passengers.

The bus wound through the cows on the street, honking frustration. I got a loving embrace from Anya for making the journey. Nona and I crammed onto the bus and waved at everyone staying in Grafskaya. When I spoke a word of English to Nona, everyone turned their heads. For the trip I was a focal point of the passenger compartment. Foreigners are rarely seen in Voronezh, and absolutely unheard of in Grafskaya. I could see in the drivers' rear mirror that he watched me for most of the way home.

I didn't hold classes so much as hold attention spans. Most students were willing to watch the teacher regardless of what the teacher was doing. I mean that, in a sense, the teacher is always right, intuitively. There are students, though, who will want to question at each breath. In the first few classes I was able to keep their attention while I plied them with my own sense of the world and my evolving understanding of Russia.

Most of my students were from Voronezh and only a handful had travelled much outside. A few students, whose parents were in the army, had travelled extensively, they had come great distances to finally settle in Voronezh. Liza was from Tajikistan and Elena had crossed the entire empire from Khabarovsk. Two students, Kalina and Luba, had come from the Pacific port city of Vladivostok. Each time I had a new class, I placed my world map up on the wall and had the students mark their birthplace.

Sasha was holding the phone against his chest as I entered the office.

'The word is out Brant, a native English speaker is in town,' he said in a loud whisper.

'And what does that mean? Do I have to leave?' I asked. 'Beat him up?'

Sasha put the phone to his ear and said a few affirming words then hung up.

'It seems the university has heard you are here. They would like to have you come by. I think they will try and steal you from us.'

'Steal, you mean I'm a commodity? Why do they need me? I am just learning how to teach here, I don't think I'm ready for a university. What university is it?' I asked.

'The State University of the Russian Federation,' Sasha said.

'I'd rather blind myself with a fork.'

'What?'

'It's an old prairie cliché... portaging.'

The phone rang and Sasha picked it up. I stood in a trance. My entire life's academic profile flashed before my eyes. Here I was, just a guy who had decided to teach in a small Russian city. It was my love for travelling that made me choose Russia and it was teaching that became my means. I was becoming a better teacher, day by day, but teaching at a university, certainly one that belonged to the Russian Federation, seemed doomed. This had a strange hierarchy aspect to it. It was a huge offer. If I managed to make it through, if I could just gather the shards of my confidence and hold them for a few months, I would leave Russia with far more experience than I'd ever hoped for.

Sasha did some confirming grunts and hung up. 'They want to see you today'.

'Sasha,' I stuttered and wrung my hands, 'Do you think-' I stopped. I realized Sasha couldn't see I was governed by fear and trepidation. I knew I hid those traits well. So, I asked him what implications this would have on my teaching at the Institute.

It was then Sasha told me of an unseen battle involving English speakers and he educated me on the politics of such rare creatures. He told me the University would snatch me and hold me, then force me to teach and teach and teach for them until I no longer had anything to do with Sasha or his Institute. Sasha didn't want to give me up, not an inch. My fear rose to where I clutched my clothes.

'Really?' I said concerned.

'Really,' Sasha said, ever poised to answer the phone. 'I will come with you but we must make damn sure they don't steal you. You are our asset.'

'A valuable one?'

'Yes, very valuable.'

I loosened the grip on my clothes and put my feet on the desk.

Sasha and I walked to the State University of the Russian Federation. The main doors opened onto Prospect Revolution and opposed the Koltsovsky Park's semi-green semi-turf. The exterior was nothing much to look at. It was just a five-storey building that ran along the street. It was neither academically intimidating nor skillfully charming in an educated sense. It was just a set of doors like so many others along the street.

Inside there were streams of students dashing to classes. The wide halls and staircases were filled with people racing to and fro, up and down. Sasha knew where we were headed and sometimes we were tethered only by glances. The Linguistics Department was far away. There were four staircases and many halls. The interior was definitely a school, replete with bells, course schedules, perky young students, and grim looking teachers.

A perquisite of teaching is every now and again you find yourself in the teachers' lounge. I felt like I'd been upgraded to business class. Sasha and I waited in the lounge for a teacher who was just wrapping up a class. We were treated to chai and left to look through school newsletters.

'The tea is just a tactic,' said Sasha, 'Don't think they are being nice.'

'I won't,' I said, 'But it is good tea.'

'No it isn't. It's the cheap stuff.'

Luba entered the room with a satchel bursting with school-like material. She was stunningly attractive and I felt Sasha look at me as if her appearance was another ploy. I didn't think Luba was a ploy and if she was, who cared. She had an accent that was the finest I had ever heard. It was a heart-stopping mix of Russian and Scottish. She confided that she'd learned all her English in Voronezh from a Scottish teacher. I was beginning to like the university. We got down to business. It seemed there were six hundred English students on the campus. They were currently all being taught by Russian teachers and the presence of a native English speaker could greatly affect the students' determination and grades. I wasn't expected to teach all six hundred but I was asked if I could help the more important classes, those nearing the end of their schooling. I was asked if

I could spare time to teach and train the fifth and sixth years. I could develop the lessons, tests and hold classes as I saw fit. Sasha's foot started to twitch. The final grade in the school is the sixth and it would be a benefit if I could work with them in their final year. If there was time, I could work with the fourth years as well. Sasha cleared his throat. Never had I thought I'd be offered such a position with such freedom. Sasha was probably denying everything she said. To him, it was rivalry. To me, it was opportunity. I agreed to teach the fifth and sixth years a few nights a week. Sasha broke in and said we, as a collective, would get back to her with the particulars. With that we left Luba and walked back to the Institute.

On a murky Saturday morning, I was taken to a vodka picnic. In two dusty Ladas, the faculty drove out to a special place where they liked to conduct their drinking ceremonies. Along the way, I asked if there was any chance I could drive. I griped that I didn't know when I'd have the chance again. (If God put me on this earth for two reasons, one was to drive. I'm still trying to figure the other one out, but it might involve pottery.) Oleg, who was an advisor to the ultra-leftist federal candidate for Russian president Vladimir Zhirinovsky, pulled the Lada to the side of the road. He smelt like vodka already. I jumped into the drivers' seat and slid the car off the curb. I was in my glory to be motoring down a lonely highway. I could have driven to Tatarstan but Oleg did several hand signals and directed me off the road. We pulled on to a small path that, judging by the depth of leaves, was seldom used. We passed between trees and drove behind cabins. There was water nearby and mist curled through the forest. Within a half-hour of leaving town, we were in the middle of a remote forest on a lazy riverbank. There was no one else around. It was peaceful and serene until Oleg started playing his tape deck at uber-treble. Eight of us looked for wood and built a large fire. Lucia and I giggled as a proclamation poem, one intended to wish us a good drunk, was read by Elena the secretary.

I wish you died...

But not now, rather when you are 120 years old.

And not in your own bed, but in the bed of your lover.

And not from a heart attack, but from the knife of her husband.

And not just like that, but for a REASON.

Everyone looked to me for my absorption. 'Hmm. To non sequitor in *all* its multicultural charm!' I said raising my glass. Everyone toasted. I was anointed with a sixth shot of vodka before I went off in search of more firewood. In the intensity of the birch woods, I stood mesmerized. Never had I felt so remote, so alone. I wandered along the bank of the river and skipped stones into the reeds, scattering a pair of mating ducks. My heart felt wild, reckless, and above all else, free. I was answerable to no one. My very being was surrounded by thousands of miles of rural freedom, my motherland. And my throat was burning.

For nine hours, vodka and cabbage pie fueled me. Deals were forged to smuggle Oleg and Vladimir into Canada in coffee containers. Vodka dipped around plastic cups and music whined from a Lada's speaker. The fire pit was stoked to life again and again. I wandered back to skipping stones alone. I savored the moment and wanted it to last. With my heart filled with song and my head filled with prancing visions of a personal utopia, I was struck by a Russian frisbee. Oleg had missed catching this rather heavy device that had knocked loose my hold on gravity.

'Brant got hit by frisbee!' Marina yelled.

'That isn't a frisbee… it's a fucking discus,' I moaned. I bled quite a bit and thought I managed an aquarium for awhile but in the spirit of, well… more vodka, I healed pretty quick.

All ten of us were *hammered*, a term I had to explain to the crowd. Hammered, inebriated, intoxicated, shitfaced, gone, smashed, under the influence, pissed, tanked, liquored, drunk, section thirty-two dash eight…however you measure it, some 25 bottles of vodka met their demise in the woods that after-noon. The day wrapped up when the sun settled beyond the opposing bank and the fire could not stave off the evening's chill. The designated driver was passed out in a pile of leaves. As Alina met the criteria by balancing on one foot for the long-est, she drove. Russian roads are treacherous for this reason. I have seen men too drunk to operate their door handles still drive. With the wife and kids in the car they drove. With a drink in hand they drove. It is a sad cultural detail that alcohol sends more people to their graves in Russia than any other country. Drinking is a right and driving a privilege. If the militsia stops you, you can buy your way out of trouble. If you get stopped because you wrapped your car around a police car, you can buy your way out of that too.

Anya began spending more and more time with me. Her bus left two hours after classes ended and that time had, prior to my arrival, been spent at Nona's. Now Anya spent the time with me. She loved to clean and cook. I hated both. With her I began a page of Russian words and phrases. She was reluctant to speak English and as I developed my Russian, we spoke predominantly Russian. One page grew into many and my Russian developed rapidly.

It was only November but Anya had squeezed into my life

with permanence. If it weren't for the student/teacher problem, it would have been an instant and intense romance. She was 22, beautiful, with no real knowledge of the outside world. She could be shown the world beyond Voronezh. But our respective positions at the school were reinforced every time I saw her at her desk in class. I agonized over what would happen to my teaching career. It was an intricate secret, one we vowed not to leak. I then learnt Nona learned about everything we did. And Nona confided in her roommate.

One evening, while Anya slaved away at my stove boiling meat and baking potato cakes for my dinner, Lucia happened. I was walking home with her after classes. I liked her Italian accent in her French. The stars were bright and spinning. We were talking about the things we missed on the 'outside' when she looked at me with these sexy don't-fuck-with-me-I'm-Italian eyes and sucked my teeth for ten minutes, right there on Plexhanovskaya Street. Our westernized pasts and the French connection were commonalities and they drew us together. That kiss moved the goal posts. However, when she made motions to my flat I had to stop her. I feigned an aggressive sleepy attack and arranged whatever was to come for the following night. If Lucia knew about Anya, the whole thing would fall apart into stupid little pieces. I thwarted Lucia, initiated a goodnight kiss and bounced back from her with '*Demaine soir madame-moiselle…*'

E.B. White said 'English usage is sometimes more than mere taste, judgment and education. Sometimes it's sheer luck, like getting across the street.' I found confidence in this statement. It gave me room to maneuver. You can't learn English from a dictionary. You need experience, guidance, and luck.

In an effort to show my students I understood what they were going through, I printed a page from a Russian news site, took it to my classes, and attempted to read the article. In addition, I had them translate what I was saying. They were to decipher my Russian and turn it into English. If all went well, I would read with precision and every student would have an identical copy. I sucked. Russian is an especially hard language to read. Your tongue has to be an acrobat and there is no net. The students found it hard to interpret what I was saying. There were laughs, snickers, and lulls of silence. Beneath the embarrassment I endured came a connection, something that told the students it was okay to make mistakes; it was okay to fail but you have to try.

I entered the office one afternoon. Sasha turned his chair.

'How are you this day?' he asked.

'I just ate five ginseng roots. Wanna play chess?'

'Actually I have a question for you.'

'I'm all ears.' I said.

'Good God! What does *that* mean?'

'It's Canadian for 'I'm listening.'' I said.

'Would you like to teach privately?' he asked.

'Tutor?' I bounced back. 'What level?'

'Intermediate. He's a friend of a friend,' Sasha said, 'Quite bright.'

My teaching skills were budding. I was just becoming accustomed to groups of eyes on me. There was finally comfort instructing a crowd but I had never really thought of private lessons. This was because in many countries it was frowned upon, illegal, or punishable by deportation with no chance of visiting the country again. The school you worked for had priority and technically *owned* your teaching skills. But here was my boss, asking me to share my talents with a friend of a friend.

'All right' I said, without any stress on the words. While I thought through the hours in my days not yet filled, Sasha swung open the door and there stood my student.

'Sergei… Brant, Brant… Sergei.'

Sergei was the root design of all male Russians. His nose was broad and long and eclipsed by lips that frowned when he smiled. His eyes darted around. He was humbled to be meeting *the* English teacher who could help make his dreams come true. Sergei was dressed tight in winter clothes. After a handshake, he began disrobing to a comfortable layer. It wasn't cold enough to warrant what he enveloped himself in. Sergei had no snaps, he was all buttons and where the button had gone astray, there were safety pins. Sasha and I waited while Sergei fought with his clothes.

'So you would like to take some English classes Sergei?' I offered to break the silence.

'Da, da… English. You teach,' he said, working hard at his clothes.

I determined, as Sergei turned and spoke to Sasha in Russian, that Sergei was not at an intermediate level. Sergei's English was poor and he chose to have Sasha translate.

Sasha nodded his head in their discussion. 'Sergei would like to study with you once a week. He says if that is okay with you.'

I agreed. Then came the fee. They spoke low as Sergei worked at freeing his fingers from his gloves. I would have agreed on any amount. I wasn't in Russia for the money, certainly not Russian wages, but I figured a few weeks of this one-on-one would prepare me for real money in the future. What if Sergei didn't approve of me? What if he saw I was just a regular guy who spoke English? I had to remember I was in every sense of the word a teacher. I was a native English speaker. I was over-qualified for once in my life and worth every damned ruble. Sasha explained to me that Sergei was a computer programmer and that America was offering jobs by the hundreds to those amazingly proficient Russians who spoke

English. Furthermore, there was a firm in Colorado that had been drawing on the talents of Voronezh. Sergei needed to be able to conduct himself through a phone interview in English. This interview was to take place in two months time. I had my work cut out for me.

'Three hundred rubles for two hours, once a week.' Sasha said. Sergei looked on waiting for confirmation. I was speechless. This was a stupendous amount. I agreed on the wage and to Sundays at noon. Sergei was visibly pleased. He put his hat on and walked out unbuttoned.

'He wants to be as fluent like me,' Sasha said.

'That will take years, maybe more.' I said.

'English is easy. Once you have the foundations, everything goes simply. It is not science rocket.'

'No...' I said, preparing to leave, 'It... isn't that.'

The temperature dropped below zero and the first ear-flap Russian fur hats (called *ushanka*) came out on the same day. The wind was straight. No currents, just razor sharp and biting. I got home from the Institute at the dark hour of 1800. Anya was cooking dinner for me. She wasn't in class earlier. The disappearance of her family's car had turned her world inside out. Her grandparents now had no way to get the cow's milk to the market. She was stressed out and I offered sanctuary in my apartment after listening to the latest 'missing-Lada' inconveniences.

After dinner, she asked me if I'd walk her to the train station, two kilometers away. It was frightfully cold but I couldn't say 'No, it's frightfully cold' to a woman who gets off at an unlit concrete platform with no ride to meet her. It did cross my mind but I doubled up my socks and threw on my scarves. We started walking briskly to the north.

And then... the moon flickered, nearly full from behind a hammer and sickle fence. The wind swept a sooty smoke into my lungs from a nearby fire and I thought 'It's autumn in Russia!' I raised my arms and inhaled with flared nostrils, then glimpsed at Anya, looking at me as if I was about to experience an unpleasant culture shock.

Beating my chest, I said 'Smell that Anya... ahh!'

From the Cyrillic lettering on the fence, I enunciated 'Crem-it-or-ium'. Burning bodies?! It was the single most appalling few seconds of my life. Death blew around me and filled my lungs with other people's DNA. I choked and spit while drawing crosses in the air. I will forever be suspicious of smoke.

Twenty minutes later we entered the train station - the shrine of distance. We ran for the terminus, dodging the ever-present babushkas. It was a peculiar cold inside the cavernous Vauxhall; it was more musty body heat condensing than anything coming from the mounted radiators. Arm in arm we climbed the stairs to the platform. I was standing in a movie. Anya's train was steaming and venting to the left. Guards in their long Russian greatcoats smoked ahead of us, nodding in conversation. An incoming train slid off to the left tracks with its train horn and squealing brakes echoing off the station walls. Old women hobbled up and over the tracks with their plastic bags. I glanced at Anya. She was beautiful and young. But after years of climbing across the rails, in these temperatures, she too will be crevassed and split; toothless and hunched. There were drunkards in their caps heading for the front of the train where the drunks and smokers have to sit. There were sulfur lights flickering down the rail beds and there was that camouflage Soviet-green covering the carriages. Everyone was breathing vapor trails into the wind. Nothing was out of character. Our words were scripted; we were just delivering them. The train blasted its horn, a nasty attendant hollered departure and Anya climbed into the cold shell of the second wagon. I watched it stammer ahead, locking the couplers and pull into the rails out. Running up the concrete steps of the catwalk, I saw the single light in the rear wagon slide away. The lights of Voronezh sat buoyant off to my right.

Russia has a perplexing charm. That particular ten minutes standing on the platform was all acted out in perfect time. I saw something Anya could not. The people in Voronezh have a hard time understanding certain moments here are captivating and magical to a foreigner. These are the same trains they rode in the 1960s, the same buildings, only in worse repair, they waited in with their parents. And maybe I do know why they can't accept it. I had ten minutes of something that certifies me as being in Russia and Anya, a true Russian, was soon to be braving a cold and dark night crossing miles of fields to get to her home. Maybe my Russia isn't really Russian.

I was picked up as I hitchhiked across town. I began my usual stumble through the question of 'How much to my home on Koltsovskaya?'

As I climbed in, Natasha, the driver, stated she didn't want any money for the trip. In fact, she pulled out a money clip of American twenty dollar bills while digging for her lighter. It was her boyfriend's car and he could, she suggested, fill it. Natasha was studying English at the pedagogical university in the city. This, I noted, was where my boss had been educated.

'Small world,' I commented then muttered, 'Small town.'

In exchange for the ride in her rusty Lada Signet, she asked if I'd speak to her in English for awhile. She held such a fawn-like aura of innocence that I found it hard to look in her eyes because she stole my confidence. Her body could wreck a happily married heart. I agreed to help her with her English, it was the least I could do for the ride. She dropped me off at my complex and said she'd pick me up at eight that night.

At eight precisely, the hideous doorbell rang. I welcomed

her in for a brief look at my flat. It must have looked quite exotic to a regular Russian. I had a line of travel and science books held in place by an ancient globe bookend. There was a cabinet where I'd displayed every colourful card I'd received from home. Maps of Canada, Russia, and the world were stapled into the wall-carpets. My laptop hummed an incandescent glow. Natasha was not a regular Russian and her quick browse ended with a quick 'hm!' in C sharp. I had planned on staying at my flat but she insisted on holding our 'lesson' at a restaurant. We swept down the stairs and climbed into her boyfriend's Lada.

The *Otlichniki Zona* on Prospect Revolution was a small red door on the main street. This led down a flight of pine stairs. Natasha suddenly seemed to have a definite authority. She spoke with flare, elegance, and demand. She told the two tough Armani-clothed men flanking the foot of the stairs to fetch someone and not to dawdle. A woman appeared and Natasha asked for, what I presumed to be, her regular table. The woman clasped her hands, held them to her chest with a slight bow and said *'Konyeshna'* (of course). The Armani linebackers took our coats.

We entered a piece of mafia-heaven; it was, I instantly knew, the finest bar/restaurant in town. It was bright and lively; people were laughing, drinking, shouting and tipping the waitresses large American bills. The walls were red brick with burnt cedar beams running along the ceiling. There was a Christmas tree, a short and unattractive thing, in the center. This was my first real experience with *New Russians*. With the collapse of the Soviet Union, many people became entrepreneurs overnight. If you were extremely rich and smart, you bought up the state's property and became an oligarch. If you weren't that rich or that smart but you still found a niche to fill and it gave you substantially greater income than you ever dreamt possible, you became a New Russian. If you extorted money from either, you were mafia.

Natasha ordered for me, something no one had done since I was eight years old. I was full but it is inhospitable to show up at such a restaurant with the lame excuse that you'd eaten four baguettes.

'There is always room for caviar.' The waitress stayed at our table for ten minutes while Natasha flipped through the menu asking various questions about the items. Ten minutes. Natasha ordered crepes, chicken salads, two spicy drinks apiece and by my special request, melted cocoa over imported chocolate ice cream. Natasha herself was the proverbial Russian 'riddle wrapped in a mystery inside an enigma'. She asked if we could see the dance floor.

'Konyeshna' agreed our waitress.

In a narrow room perhaps forty people clothed in expensive suits and dresses were partying it up in this underground club. The women were all model-material, and the men all looked foreign, and were in town on business. I wasn't dressed to dance or fit in; I was a visual conflict. I had on a Vancouver Canucks hockey jersey with my name on the back. Besides I only have one dance step and I like to save it for when I'm drunk.

For all the time I'd spent in Voronezh, I had never expected I would see something like this, a place where money gathered. None of my students could have afforded to dine in the *Otlichniki Zona*. And that made me feel uncomfortable. As Natasha encouraged me back to the table, she started to part with the truth.

'Brant, there is much money in Russia.' She smiled like 'crime' was implicit but too delicate or obvious to mention. I looked around and saw that there were cell phones everywhere. A cell phone was extraordinarily expensive in Russia.

And you can't rent one. I told her I knew you couldn't rent anything.

We ate our caviar, drank our strange spicy drinks, and worked through the warm cocoa on ice.

'Russia is a baby,' Natasha started. 'Russia is old, da… but Russia is like a baby now. It will have a very strong future I think. Now, it walks like it is trying to for its first time. It falls this way and that but it will soon stand. I think Russia in the next hundred or so years will be the best place in the world.'

'I hope that's true,' I said. I wanted Russia to be strong; I wanted an economy where every Russian could afford to spend the occasional night in a restaurant of the *Otlichniki Zona*'s quality.

'Things just take time. Since I won't be here to enjoy it, I must enjoy what I can now.' She pulled her trademark smile, probably the one that attracted her boyfriend, and twinkled. Nothing she had said had explained herself. Why, for instance, did she have rolls of American bills and a wardrobe that styled her better than anyone I'd seen in Voronezh? But I couldn't yet approach that issue with tact.

'How did this bar get built?' I asked. She looked at me like Condé Nast had done a spread on it and I hadn't gotten my copy. There was no mystery her eyes said.

'Moscow businessmen keep their money in Voronezh. It is safe here. When they come here to see it, they want to have a good time.'

That didn't really answer my question so I asked how something like this could exist in a country that is the opposite. And the local banks hadn't won any Michelin awards with me so I was still confused. This was something you would expect in Moscow. I tried not to be confrontational and offered her avenues of escape, which she used.

'Brant. Russian businessmen do their meetings in *banya*.

They sit in the sauna, drink lots of vodka, and business gets done.' Then in Russian she said, 'Understand?'

Foreign accents knock me out of orbit. She could have been 280lbs of varicose veins and missing her ears but with that accent she owned me. I was developing a strange and respectful feeling for Natasha and it was a specific emotion, one built just for her.

A party on the landing just a few steps up broke out into the English birthday song with an uproarious *'Xappy bet-day to you, xappy bet-day to you...'*

'The people only know a few English songs, words or cliché phrases. I was at a Blues concert last night,' Natasha said. 'The band was from Saint Petersburg. And when they had finished their playing, and what beautiful playing it was, they yelled 'Thank You! Thank You!' to the audience in English. The audience yelled back 'You are welcome!'

I looked perplexed. She continued while moving her straw through the margarita foam in her glass.

'They don't speak English. They only know that it is the language that they'd love to master,' she said. I soon understood. For Russians, yelling 'You are welcome' is no different from 'Encore!', 'Gesuntheit', or 'Hasta la vista' for English speakers. We use them the same way that the New Russians are using our language. It is to sound a bit *haute-cultured*, to show they are worldly and to have some connection, however tenuous, to the language of the world.

Our bill was a month's wage and Natasha was culturally-offended that I even thought of covering it. I didn't offer to pay all of it actually, only mine, specifically the ice cream. I realized that my financial situation didn't permit me to dine there. My wages were high for Russia but this strange underworld place was for a different crowd altogether. It was for the prosperous New Russians and the elite mafia boys who could afford to talk endlessly on their cell phones like Westerners on an 'unlimited evenings' plan. I wondered how many of them washed their clothes in the bathtub.

Natasha drove me home in the starry night. As she puttered out of my complex I wondered at it all. I was under the delusion this was language work, a study of English. I couldn't risk anything with Natasha. I was having problems keeping Anya and Lucia straight. No, I would tell Natasha that I could no longer meet and share tables of food with her. I would stop anything before romance reared itself.

As I mounted the stairs, I chuckled to myself. If her boyfriend ever found out about me… I stopped myself there or I wouldn't get to sleep. I had already conjured him up. He'd be huge, with an alpha-dog irritability in a designer suit. He'd fiddle with his rings and crack his knuckles. People would have names for him. I decided to put an end to it before anyone got hurt. I opened the door to my flat and the orange phone rang. It was Natasha; she'd had such a nice time that she invited me out on Saturday.

'Sure,' I said. My brain isn't always in gear before my mouth is in motion. I agreed to lunch on the weekend.

Lucia and I repeatedly came into contact with a woman whom we'd named 'KGB-chick' due to her ubiquitous nature. I thought she was Lucia's friend and Lucia thought she was mine. KGB-chick spoke five languages and her English, French, and Italian, were strong enough to break apart the exclusive relationship Lucia and I had. We both resented her. Knowing we were spending time with her was like waiting for surgery. KGB-chick took us to restaurants with the purpose of gaining insight into our native countries and our pasts. But it was a needling, as if she was obtaining data. Her questions seemed rehearsed, cold and aggressive. She tried to fit herself into every activity and then began booking things for the three of us. KGB-chick told me we were going swimming. I told her no, the water has never been 'good' once I've gotten in. She asked me to go horseback riding but I declined explaining I had hemorrhoids the size of Uzbek doorknobs. Just when it seemed she'd taken the hints and was going to leave us alone, she intercepted Lucia without plans after school. Lucia asked me politely to come or face the consequences.

KGB-chick took us to meet her *Latino Americana* (sic) friends. Moneza and Loneza were cousins from Ecuador and both had signed five-year contracts to study and stay in Voronezh. The two had endured three years so far, surviving in a dormitory that was unfit for living. The dark stairwell had been laced with groups of people drinking, smoking, and urinating. Ten storeys up, in a building with a few dim light bulbs, the women shared 140 square feet. This 'room' was divided by hanging sheets to denote personal space. There were eighteen such 'rooms' and one rude toilet per floor. Cigarette burns covered every square inch of the hallway linoleum and occasional missing chunks of floor exposed more missing chunks of the floors below. Drunk men were leaning against hallways mumbling about better times and people they'd beat up if they were there. The two cousins spoke Spanish. So did KGB-chick who conducted our trivial conversations for us. We ate grapes and listened to Ricky Martin tapes in mono until the refrigerator had to be plugged back in so nothing spoiled. It was a Friday night in Voronezh, where, in a city of distress, one realized that the only thing worse than pain is suffering; and the only thing worse than suffering is cabbage soup leftovers.

. . .

I started teaching classes at the Russian State University. My first day, I stood outside the double doors afraid to enter. I grasped the big handle and found it locked. The adjacent door swung open and a stream of students collected outside for cigarettes. Walking into the front foyer, I entered into chaos and the slow entropy of my brain. There were students anxiously running about with satchels and books. I grabbed a worn banister that led to the first level. Standing at the top of that set of stairs were two security guards, one thankfully spoke some French he'd picked up in the war. This kind gentleman took the time to draw me a map to the classroom, after frisking me.

'Merci!' I said and waved.

'We surrender!' he yelled back.

Though I'd been there once, none of my memories materialized to guide me. It is a vast university. This was the artillery of the government. It was education with unparalleled volume. I wondered at all of the students and teachers, at their relationships. I felt like a new bicycle at an airshow. The guard's map was sufficient to get me onto the wrong floor twice, from two different directions. Finally, I stumbled into my class. There were thirty students in mid-sentence as I entered. I pulled a long confident smile and felt vomit rise in my throat. Three of those present were teachers I recognized. This was the big time. This was my shot at the scoreboard. At the front of the classroom was a podium. A god damn podium! I made my way in great strides and settled my knapsack at my feet.

'Ok, put on your game face,' I thought to myself.

A woman in the last row asked what a 'game face' was. I smiled at her. With my hands clutching the corners of the stand, I started my introduction, playing out who I was and why I was there. I pulled out my frequently-used map and splayed it across the board. I detailed British Columbia's forestry practices, the Vancouver film scene, my home's proximity to America, and

Canada's common northern climes with Russia. My father works in tourism and he had sent me a videotape of a tourism plug for Vancouver. I'd never seen it and asked if there was a video player to watch it on. A young woman from the back said something in Russian and left. She returned with a TV/VCR on a cart. I could smell cigarette smoke. I slipped the tape in and pressed play. I was stunned. When I saw the montage of my home I wanted to be there. I wanted to water-ski and downhill ski in the same afternoon.

I wanted to ride bareback in the surf. I wanted to charter a helicopter and clip the skids on my city's peaks. So, too, did my class. It was influential and inviting. It ran 12 minutes. Question time came around.

'Are you married?' they asked.

'No' I said.

'Are you single?'

'… yes,' I managed, choosing the option to keep it simple.

'Are you gay?'

'… no, I am not gay. I'm curious as to why that question always follows the other two. It's as if-'

'Do you have any children?'

'No. Fiscally, I cannot have children. I talked to an accountant at the mall and she said I am unable.'

'Are you a religious man?'

'It isn't all a+b=c… something bigger is going on.'

'Is Hollywood a beautiful place?'

'Ninety-five percent of Hollywood is a hole in the ground; it is dirty, poor and nothing at all like you probably think it is. And you can't get into the other five percent. You ask a cop for directions and he runs your plates. You ask a Latino homeboy for directions and he runs your plates. Next.'

'What about Las Vegas?'

'I got $281 in parking fines on a 'quick' trip to Vegas…

that, unfortunately, was my only 'sin'. I'm the wrong person to ask. Next.'

'Do you miss anyone at home?' they asked.

'I miss Shasta, my Cocker Spaniel. Everything I know about enthusiasm, I learned from him. I brought a picture. See? Yep, pass it around… my best bud… but he's getting old. He looks the same but it keeps getting easier to sneak up on him.'

'What do you like most about Russia?'

'I love Russia. She is my soul mate. I was in Leningrad and Moscow when I was five years old. I've lived in Estonia and taken the railway across Siberia. Russia is in my system. I like the good guys and the bad guys. Stalin's ice-picking of Trotsky half a world away… you've indeed lived in interesting times. If that happened in Canada, we'd have to close the country down so we could look inside ourselves and wonder where our ideology went wrong… and then we'd all have to register our ice picks. In Russia, it's just another day. I love your authors, your poets, your composers, that whole thing with Rasputin. I see magic in your history, for good or bad. I love the things you hate. I even like taking the tram.'

'Do you love anything else?'

'The cost of CDs.'

'Your feelings come across as warm and sincere. How do you feel about Chechnya?'

'Oh… that,' I said scratching my two-day old goatee and evaluating my reply. 'Well let me just say that I think… the Chechnyans have a point. Next question please.'

'Do you support their cause?'

'Please, I am against war in all forms,' I said. 'I don't even like hunting. I was in Wyoming with men who like to get drunk and shoot three-foot holes into six-inch animals for fun.'

'Did Hitler have a *point*?'

'Oh for the love of God... can somebody please ask me if I like sunsets or caviar?'

These are fifth year English students and they read Dante, translated Pushkin, and used five-dollar words to describe themselves. They were quite a sophisticated match. It was during this interlude I became aware of the lack of males in the classrooms, in the halls, anywhere. I had one twenty-something guy in the room, far at the back. The rest were women.

One woman asked what I thought about Putin. Her voice was an instrument, she sang when she spoke. I answered I held no political views in Russia; that I came squeeky apolitical, and I tried to change the subject. Russian politics and religion are electric. If I say something, I would be branded a certain way, and from that I fragment into assumptions. Sure I had individual thoughts on Russia and Stalin, Chechnya, communism, and the collapse of the Soviet Union but to divulge my perspectives could illicit conversations that might have me fired or possibly worse – secretly 'removed'. I didn't want to sway views with my BBC.com education. I wanted, if anything, to gain politics and religion from the people I met. I wanted to see how Russians today came to terms with Russia's past. I resolved before coming that I was not allied with any religious denomination, political organization, institution, or sect and my open-mind policy was developed from years of learning how different people and places are.

The students wanted to sap the *American Experience* out of me, forget the Louis Riel monologue, avoid Nunavut, and leave Canada at the door. They wanted me in character, to personify exactly what I was: I was exporting culture. I merged a few stand-up comedy acts, did a scene from *Planes, Trains and Automobiles*, and a good take of George Bush and Laura when the lights went out. I regaled them with travels into Harlem, spring break in Daytona Beach, and of the stupid mistakes one can make in Amsterdam when one feels lonely. I told them of my previous employment, the things I ate, and detailed who was in my family and what they did there.

I turned the tables and discovered a peculiar fact. Russians are out of touch with Russia. These students, though educated and intellectual, were committed to living in a local - not Moscovian or global - sense. Voronezh is topical; Moscow and Russia were conceptually greater than they felt able to relate to or comment on. Most didn't know which direction Moscow was or its relationship to Saint Petersburg. Instead they knew how many nights it was to get somewhere by train, which I found poetic. The country is just too damn big said one student.

On a government form given out during a class, the students were asked to fill in the blanks. The page read as follows:

In Russia, I would like to see change _____

In Voronezh, I would like to see change _____

In the province, I would like to see change _____

On the other side was enough space to voice anything not yet covered. One student wrote *'You, Vladimir K. YOU will get in... then you will lie, lie, lie, lie, lie, lie, lie, lie, lie, lie...`* on all fifteen lines. She turned it in and is probably splitting rocks in Yakutsk now. I was not given one.

I've had a bad neck for a long time. I had tried countless treatments at home and nothing, from acupuncture to chiropractors to naturopathic witch doctors, had sufficiently eased the pain. Marina said there was a doctor who specialized in injuries and I debated risking my body to a Russian doctor with Russian means. I did, finally, agree. We took multiple trolleybuses to his office. The walls of the building had been bombed. Or if it wasn't a bomb, then it was the kind of graphic decay that reason tells you is unsafe. The stiff steel railings were detached and bent out of their functional form. The steps had bricks missing and were hard to ascend. Inside the doctor's waiting room, the walls and small bench were bland, rustic and surrounded by oak doors with peeling paint. We waited a half hour beyond the appointment time then went outside for a cigarette.

In the midst of a setting ravaged by time and careless attention was an old woman burning leaves. With the archetypal homemade broom, she swept, then laid her broom aside and grasped armfuls of leaves. The moment was charming, contented, real. I could have watched her all day. It was pastoral enough to have painted this scene, her quick stabs at the pile, the cone of smoke from the barrel, and the sunlight filtering through the trees.

Marina and I returned indoors and found the doctor was still not in. We departed into the beautiful autumn air and I tipped my hat to the woman raking her pile. She noticed but didn't know what my nod meant. Perhaps she missed the beauty she was creating.

In turn, Marina took me to another doctor, a friend of hers who dabbled in chiropractics, model airplanes and massage. His office was in yet another building that looked like the Germans had just left. It was old and decrepit. Plaster had fallen from most of the front and bricks were slowly edging out of their nooks. Yakov was probably in his early thirties and he was laughingly outgoing. Within five minutes I was hoisted nude upon his bed. Marina stayed, half covering her eyes, for translation purposes.

Marina and I had picked up a package of syringes prior to coming. I was told that Russian manufactured ones may break or leak so I decided to buy Belgian ones. Yakov gave me two shots of drugs. He cracked my back the way you open a peanut and hooked me up to an electronic machine that looked like it was from an Antonov cockpit.

'UGG!' I cried as shocks ran the length of my body.

'It will be alright soon Brant.' said Marina.

'UHH!'

'Shh, try to be qui-'

'UGG!' I screamed.

'Just a few more minutes of this and you will feel better.'

'UHH!'

'You are disturbing the other people.'

'UGG!'

'Relax, it's just a… it is to relax your muscles.'

'My musc-UHH - my children will be missing electrons… UGG!'

After that, I had a full body massage and then to round out the hour, a mud bath made with imported Dead Sea mud.

I felt pretty good and Yakov encouraged me to attend ten more sessions, promising me it would work.

After working through Natasha's homework one afternoon, we embraced in a farewell bear hug that would have stilled the wind. I nestled my chin on her shoulder and smelt her mafia hair. Below, through the window, I saw a man in a long coat sprint out the door of a store and leap a fence, vaulting for a narrow space between two parked Ladas. The instant his foot hit the ground, a driver's door jerked open. He slammed into it and fell to the ground, winded. The driver jumped out and began kicking the biological stuffing out of him. Two passengers emerged and joined in, beating him mercilessly. Blood splattered on the snow.

'Look!' I pointed, unraveling from Natasha's arms. She

turned and gasped. Fearful of being seen, she grabbed my hand and tried to drag me away.

'That was, for lack of a better adjective, neat-o!' I said in the hallway.

Natasha reached for her things, 'Brant... I must go'.

'Just adding to your intrigue?' I helped her assemble her books, 'Or was that your prompt?'

'I just must go-' she said as the car retreated backwards up busy Koltsovskaya Street.

I've seen things that came close to this incident but none so watch-able, none seen from a second-storey window, none seen in Russia. Natasha's strange behavior made me wonder what she was a part of. Perhaps she knew the bloody man. Perhaps he was waiting for her? She never let on either way. I preferred to just speculate that the mafia was securing my personal perimeter while I had my way with the English language, and I let her out the door. Anya was coming soon.

During a class a young man came in and sat down at the front. He asked if I minded if he participated. I said I didn't and carried on with my lesson. Something seemed strange. The third-years, though biased for Russian, were comfortable speaking to me in English. Why, I wondered, had they stopped. The visitor at the front began asking questions. His English was superior to any student. He queried me on American foreign policy and Russian politics. Hmm, I murmured. I asked him who he was. He took the opportunity to stand and state who he was. Alyosha detailed his short life and related his dream of attending school in America. He was both forthright and arrogant. The rest of the class played with their pens or doodled in their notebooks.

The newcomer ran out the clock. Alyosha approached me

after and said he'd enjoyed the class. I wanted to ask him why he'd deprived my students of their rightful time and seemed not to care. I had worked on opening them up yet all of them, even extroverted Slava, fell silent in Alyosha's presence. I shook his hand and offered him the opportunity to revisit us, not meaning a word of it. The bell rang, we funneled out of the room and I came chest to breast with Tatyana in the hall. She knew what I was going to ask. She smiled but her mouth swept back like a frown.

'Alyosha is the President's son. I hope he was not a bother on your class.'

'Not at all! I welcomed his avid participation... bright kid, exceedingly good at English and a ... he is-'

'Enough Brant, he is pain in ass.'

'Yes he does possess a few qualities that one might find eccentric.'

Alyosha was her personal student and had been since he was a boy. It was only now that he was interacting with the staff and students of the school. He was preparing to take the *Test of English as a Foreign Language* or TOEFL in April. Class time for him was now vital. She wanted him to be with *the* native English speaker.

'With me? In all my classes?' I asked.

If, she said, that would be all right.

It was all right. It was all right for a few more classes. But when Alyosha was in the room, I couldn't get any participation from my students. Alyosha was intense, perhaps gifted, but not to a class. He challenged me on several obscure topics which led to lexicon and concepts that no one else in the class bene-fited from. I resented Alyosha. He was the myopic eyes of the school, how he judged me would be dinner conversation.

Much of the time my exercises were simple, designed for the slower people in class. Nothing I taught them was too hard for Alyosha. He did have his own linguistical problems I couldn't address in my classroom. The time came when I eased up to Tatyana and asked her to remove Alyosha. She did so immediately. She asked if I could work with him at all, at any other times. His father, who was my boss, wanted Alyosha to pass TOEFL so he could study abroad in America. Faced with that fact and Tatyana's tired eyes, I conceded. I would meet Alyosha every Saturday and we would walk the town speaking English.

Plexhanovskaya Street is one of the most sensuous streets in Voronezh. Aside from the fact that it carries many cars, trams, and diesel choking buses, every weekend it becomes a long stretched out market where people, usually pensioners, come to display and sell their belongings. Since Voronezh is fairly unknown to tourists, the items for sale aren't expensive but they are magical finds. Heirlooms from past generations lined the sidewalks from Koltsovskaya to Prospect Revolution. There are vinyl records with Cyrillic covers. Chains, pins and pendants, once worn to perhaps the ballet or symphony, were now sold to buy food. There were vendors with thousands of postcards, all used and many from other countries, showing generations of postmarks. Books were strewn around. Physics textbooks and romance novels sat dog-eared and tattered. The richest part was the old men selling lapel pins, shoulder boards or stamps. Some items commemorated Voronezh or Peter the Great but most were Soviet-era Lenins and Stalins. Many were anniversary editions of the CCCP while still others honoured the achievements in aviation, space, or ocean going vessels. The stamps, too, were special and likely hard to find elsewhere. There were issues of Marx, Engels, Lenin, and revolutions past. Pushkin, Gagarin, and Tchaikovsky sets reached as far back as the forties and fifties. There they were, for sale in a weathered old pensioner's collection.

Every Saturday, Alyosha and I would try to get by and see what was new on the street. Sometimes I would spend hours going through postcards from the 1930s or thumbing vinyl records for something worth sending home. I purchased Dostoevsky's *Crime and Punishment* for a future time when my proficiency allowed me to read it in Russian. Alyosha had a passion for Russia's military and had a better grasp of his country's history than anyone else I'd met. He glorified particular artifacts with such enthusiasm that I bought them all, intent on hoarding the greatest collection of Russian memorabilia outside the country.

In Moscow, the whole Soviet Union era is on the auction block. One can buy uniforms for every rank replete with hat, chevrons, and medals. You want a pilot's license? A gas mask? A flak-jacket? A WWII walkie-talkie? A shirt that says 'McLenins'? You can buy anything from monocles to tank tracks. But in Voronezh, it was different. Their goods were personal. The prices were so low I frequently paid more to the person selling, simply to feel better for taking their history.

I began to gather names for a home schooled English class. I planned to teach six or eight people in my flat. I had so far lined up Oleg and his wife Alina. Slava, who excelled in his studies, wanted further instruction. Lucia, who didn't speak a word of the language, wanted to peek into English and decide if it was worth pursuing. I set a date in December to meet at my place. I had Lucia over one night and we talked and laughed like school children. I tried to get her to speak English but she was far too shy. This seemed to me to be rather odd since we were both speaking French which was a second language for both of us. She felt that English was so dominant, so worldly that it was beyond her reach. I picked up my Berlitz book of languages and

tried out my Italian on her. I failed miserably as one might
expect and Lucia laughed. She said 'My nem eesa Lucia'. I
laughed so hard I was coughing up chai leaves and told her
she'd done very well. Each day when I greeted her at the Institute, I would get a sharper, more correct version of 'Good day
Brant. My name is Lucia'.

I had asked, during a session with the second-year class,
how many had been on the internet. There was one hand that
confidently stayed raised. I told them of the world that awaited
them on the electronic superhighway. No one seemed to feel the
impact of my speech. The world wide web was frightening and
ungraspable. They didn't have the money to get online and if
they did, who would teach them how to use it?

I asked if the class wanted to see what life online was like. I
wanted them to see how it felt to be halfway around the world
from one's family and still feel huggably close. Late on a
Sunday afternoon, twelve second-year girls came over to see
what I was buzzing about. We couldn't just pounce on the
computer; we had first to enjoy a dinner that took three hours
and several huddles to prepare. We had to have a cake that
someone baked at home and we had to have tea. Only after all
of these formalities were they ready to see what this internet
was. I led them to my little laptop and asked them to crowd
around. First I asked for subjects and showed them how the
search engine worked. When they saw pictures of their own
rock stars, script in Russian or Voronezh sites, they were
amazed. I looked at the clock and figured my mother would be
at work in Vancouver. I wrote an email about the dinner and hit
'send'. In seconds my mother's reply bounced in. The girls
were awed. They were speechless as they read the message my
mother had typed out for them. The map was on the wall and
we all took turns pointing out that my message had just travelled to Canada and back. It was unlike anything they'd ever

experienced; they had nothing to compare it to. They were still in the old empire of the postal service.

In the next hour, I got them all email addresses. They chose cute Russian names. There, I informed them, they were all a part of the internet. They all studied their names and passwords and all stuck their little chits of paper safely away in their purses. Their problem would be finding somewhere to get online. They did have options but that was for them to discover. I had opened a door that would never close.

KGB-chick invited Lucia to the ballet. Lucia told me my attendance was inevitable. Ballet is a Russian fixation. Everyone in town goes a few times a year, even hermits and street youth, no one is exempt. We met in the cold out front of the Voronezh Ballet House and went to see 'Don Quixote'. The outside is a wonderful façade of pre-Revolutionary building. It mimics the Bolshoi in Moscow but looks more cozy and approachable. Three angels flaunt the apex and watch over the thick yellow columns. Inside, it was the theatre of theatres. There were arms of balconies and plush red velvet seats from a century back in time.

The story of Sancho and Don and the battling of windmills had a first rate set design. But ballet wasn't an art form that appealed to me. Lucia was trying to explain it in French. All I figured out was that Don was a dancer, Sancho, was a dancer and fifty other people were dancers. It was well done, whatever my interpretation. No one fell and there were many pretty women.

During the Intermission Lucia and I slipped away for a cigarette. We were told by a babushka that the smoking area was two flights down. Descending, we reached the dimly lit bowels of the theatre. There, in a squalid and rank setting, we found the entire orchestra smoking. Visibility was quickly diminished as the smoke choked out the light. No one spoke, it was just spitting and the occasional cough. The conductor threw his butt into a corner and told the others they had two minutes before the next act.

There were many book stores in the city. Books in English weren't plentiful in most of them. For the most part, school supplies and postcard racks dotted the shelves. These places liked to sell key chains and hairbrushes beside paperbacks and spy novels. There were a few stores that surprised me, a wise and seasoned book collector. One of these was *Knigi Mir*, which housed a grand assortment of books. Most of the English books were classics, ranging from 'Robinson Crusoe' to 'Anna Karenina'. They had scholastic supplies, books on tape, and language courses. The buttressed ceiling soared over the book collection and gave the establishment warmth. It had a metal detector at the door and I never failed to set it off. The 120db siren was loud enough to pop zits. You could hear people dropping books throughout the store. My Zippo proved to be the culprit. I would stroll in and set off the alarm while holding the lighter in my hand. Neither staff nor patron was quite the same after I arrived and shattered the peace.

Lucia found out about Anya and me. She came over unannounced which made it sort of her own fault. She went straight from anger to denial to acceptance and back to anger, skipping some pretty important steps of recovery. Anya didn't speak French but there was a whole lot of body language to read. I asked Anya to give us some time and turned on Lucia and lost. She spoke to herself in Italian for five minutes while rearranging the books on my shelf. I explained my side while Anya sat in the kitchen licking my stamp collection.

Lucia ignored me for two days but did not tell anyone. She knew the secret she held. But she went as far as giving the mafia code of silence with a finger to her lips and the word 'omerta', which seemed more grim than crossing her heart and hoping to die. We couldn't lose our friendship; it wasn't a bargaining chip. We needed each other. She became a sister to me. And things worked out better. We could still sit in my flat and listen to pirated Andrea Bocelli CDs. We could still have long French conversations, smoke a pack of cigarettes each, and hug each other goodbye. There just wasn't any sex. That apparently was a bargaining chip.

In every one of my classes I had at most one male. This was also true for all of Lucia's. I was amazed, for I could have up to thirty students and they were all women except the token male. I guessed the future of Russia was undoubtedly in the hands of women. The men were all off working, drunk, or in the army. The Russian army was taking young men and throwing them at Chechnya. I was walking through town one day and I met a student of mine. He was extremely worried because he was going for his recruitment examination the following day. This 'exam' would decide his fate; if he was healthy, he would go to war. He would be sent to Chechnya. The army was conscripting men for a two-year service, a term that would be hard to endure if in fact you survived it. There were years where suicide took more lives than war. This student was top of the class. None of the other students in his class were anywhere near his intellect. It would be a terrible cost to Russia to take that away from him. We parted ways, neither of us feeling too well.

Days on he appeared in class. When the corridor died down and the students left for other classes, I learned more about the situation. The student had told the panel of doctors at his examination that he had dreams of killing people. He said that sometimes he felt like killing his parents and classmates.

'Did you say anything about… your teachers?' I asked.

'No, it wasn't true. I told them all of this because I didn't want to go to war. The army in Russia is horrible. They have bad food and poor clothing. I want to do better. I am more brain than body. I can do better…'

'Did it work?' I asked.

'I did this crazy thing with my eyes! I must have acted like I wanted to kill the doctor and the nurses because he said I was not fit! Then he put a needle in my arm and I woke up at home.' He smiled wide and went home to study his English homework.

Sasha announced that he would be accompanying the school's president, Mr. Yuli Zolotovinski, to America in late November. He was excited by this news; he'd never been out of Russia.

One morning on my way to the Institute, a huge crane, hoisting a metal box of sand, toppled. It crashed down onto the fence that separates my apartment from the company that moves large boxes of sand. It broke through three concrete walls and oozed sand in every direction. It was a thunderous affair and sent children in the small garden area shrieking through the mud. Almost immediately there were men standing around scratching their heads. I slowly approached and withdrew my camera. Twenty men with white hats looked for an explanation. The tall crane itself was now not tall. The sand had just been too much stress. The men combed over the area looking for something to do.

The walls, I predicted, would remain un-repaired and the sand and the torn box from which it came were destined to be permanent fixtures of my backyard. The city looked like that was the way things were done. If something broke and could not be repaired, it was left.

Just then, a man with an orange hat came into the picture. He hollered at each man as a cooperative and threw his hand to the crane, then the sand, then the torn box, then the walls. Then he was gone. He had been very angry and I lowered my poised camera.

When I returned, four hours on, the men had nearly finished shoveling the sand. The crane was nowhere to be seen. I was wrong, Russia isn't just order into chaos, the sand people were diligent. Within two days, the walls were up and I could just see the top of a new crane swinging heavy boxes of sand.

Sergei arrived for our first class. He had tapes from an English course that he preferred to use. This was because he had listened to them over and over again but had understood and retained next to nothing. He vowed to understand the tapes. They were American, trivial and unconventional in their instruction. Sergei, however, praised them as if somehow if he came to understand the tapes, America would grant him citizenship.

I soon learned that Sergei actually had good English comprehension. He could understand the phrase but couldn't break it down into words. We worked through two hours until I was aggravated by the tapes. Sergei was eager for a second lesson. He buttoned himself up, paid for the time and left reciting something.

I had seen the last late sunsets of summer, the sweeping vistas of a spectacular autumn and then I felt the death grip of an oncoming Russian winter. Forty degrees of contrast. And it was the kind of cold that makes you shuffle everywhere, where steam pours from vents, cars need blankets stretched across their hoods and icicles threaten pedestrians.

You could see the start of paths in the snow that would guide everyone for months. Since it won't melt until March, the first snowfall is the time to crunch across parks and crease the open spaces. The snow will become ice and it will turn grey with pollution. And the only places to walk will be those paths that Voronezhians worked at designating. There had been no sand or salt spread. It was just a wacky winter wonderland. Cars went through intersections with their wheels locked and their horns blowing. You never attempted to cross a street until you saw nothing but taillights.

Despite the bad press the government, the police, and the mafia get in Russia, I felt safe in Voronezh. I had decided to stay away from dealing in arms, fissile isotopes, and drugs long before I came on the trip. The KGB or FSB may have routinely been through my apartment. Everyone I asked said that my flat would have been searched many times while I was away at school. My phone may be tapped. It would explain the static. Heavy security forces guard both the Institute and State University and they check bags and IDs everyday from people they see every day. A few times 'little' things happened while I'd been browsing the kiosks - just disorganized low-end mafia things where I got followed, and I had the foresight to leave and walk figure eights around my apartment area. Outside of that minimal contact, the city seemed no more hazardous than home.

I ended up with a lot of coins. I would frequently sneak up on a homeless beggar and fill her hat with thousands of kopeks or a bag of empty Coke Light bottles. Seniors are the people who usually recycle discarded tins and bottles. There was a return depot a few blocks from my flat and the queue could stretch a block. For each container they received a few kopeks. These weren't society's drop-outs or homeless, these were grandparents on a pension.

The saddest thing in Voronezh was the animals. Packs of stray dogs ran among the kiosks and hovered around anyone likely to drop food. They looked like road kill. One day I came across a mangy puppy trying to walk while enduring a seizure. I squatted and winced but couldn't bring myself to touch it, a compassion it sorely needed. It fell and got up and shook and fell and got up. I couldn't watch it. That is what you did there. You avoided the unpleasantness and soon enough something else disturbing will happen and you'll have forgotten it.

I sent off emails home with opinions of Russia that twelve years ago would have had me building a railroad in the north. Yet no one has came knocking except the drunk next door and it was only forty rubles to shut him up. There are more problems with drunks than anything else. It's a national problem. You can get beer or vodka easier than good drinking water. People drink inside the shopping centers and shops. They drink on the roads or in the parks. Sadly, young kids can be seen drinking in sheltered corners, huddling around a shared cigarette. When I went on a trip outside the city environs one morning, we stopped into a coffee restaurant and three men were drinking beer at eight a.m. I pointed it out. Marina looked over her shoulder at them and said, 'Yeah, but it's not vodka.'

'But they're lorry drivers,' I said.

'Yeah, but it's not vodka.'

One morning I left Voronezh before sunrise on my first visit to another of the Institutes' branches. It was planned that I would meet with all of the first year English students in the city of *Stara Oscol*. Marina and I left town in a VAZ school van driven by Mtchsht (I never learned how to pronounce it.)

In a dimly lit fog, we made our way through Voronezh's

southern districts. A tank memorial for those who fought in the Second World War stood at the edge of town. The war was still unbelievably fresh and the opponents were not referred to as Germans or even Nazis but more personably as *those Fascists.* Since the war ended, 58,000 landmines have been found around Voronezh. Hikers or farmers still accidentally found these live munitions resulting in fewer hikers and farmers.

As I'd only had a warm cup of tea in my flat, I persuaded Mtchsht to pull over at a small coffee house *and* to start smoking again. The sky was pure grey after two weeks of November sun. The road was two lanes wide but without lines to guide and separate traffic. We overtook tractors on blind curves. There were horse drawn carts piled with hay, broken down Ladas, and army vehicles along the way. It was a rolling countryside with numerous forests of birch and fields of beet-root, corn stalks, and wheat. We were pulled over at two check-points. The Russian guards, with their long coats, polished boots, truncheons, and intimidating weaponry, approached. Mtchsht got out, went through paperwork, and climbed back in.

'What did they want?' I asked.

'Dyengi...' the driver said. Money.

We arrived in the industrial capital of the Kursk province, *Stara Oscal,* after a few hours. It is a city of 250,000 people. The perimeter of the city was walled with Soviet apartment blocks, dozens of ten storey buildings. Then we were down-town and at the Institute's door. We got out into a cool breeze and entered the building.

The typical Russian University class is ten people, twelve max, to best benefit each of the students. I was comfortable with smaller classes because they had faces and individual iden-tities. I opened the door to every English student in the school, a faceless mass of teenagers in their first-year of English. It must be understood that native English speakers never come to these remote places. These cities are too far off the map for anyone from outside the country. On each face sat a big smile and eyes and ears intent on every word I said. I hung up the map of Canada, explained my purpose, my travels, my respect for their country, and why I was in Stara Oscal.

Marina burst into the room and said a TV crew was waiting for an interview.

'A what?'

'Please...' she said throwing her arm toward the door.

There were lights and nose powders, cameras and recorders, sound booms and hovering teachers from other classes. There was a cute woman with short black hair, a bad sweater, and a giant microphone. Beside her was a guy flicking switches on a huge camera. Marina translated the questions and the answers. They asked what I liked about the city which I hadn't really seen... *'I'm lucky enough to have caught it in autumn'*. Then whether or not I thought the students were gifted... *'They show promise'*. And what are my plans are for a return to the city... *'I would love to return to work with the students very soon'*.

I went back into the classroom. The camera man came in to tape for awhile.

'Ignore him...' said the teacher.

'Ignore? His camera is the size of a Volvo. And he keeps tripping on his cables.'

I carried on about my eagerness to teach in the Institute's branches, some fist-waving for Canadian hockey, and a plug for travel to Vancouver. Then it was question period. Whenever I said I was single at the advanced age of 31, the room went into whisper-mode and the smiles got bigger. Someone always queried, 'Do you like Russian girls? Yes?' Then some astute person consistently bothered to bring up the issue of my sexuality to be sure we were all flying the same flag.

None of the women liked my Lada stories. (I've owned two

Ladas in Canada. And though I was particularly fond of my 4x4 Niva, they were both useless vehicles. The first time I tried going off-road, I got stuck in a puddle. When I took it for a drive in America, the head gasket blew. Since no one on American soil had ever seen a Niva, they had no parts and no solution except to drive 300 miles home, filling up my radiator with water from a cooler and a cup every twenty miles). The only male chuckled. 'Da, da'

'Has anything in Russia shocked you yet?' asked the teacher.

I had to be careful because saying that the cockroaches were horrid or that I don't much care for squatters wasn't wise. To say that most of the public toilets were reason enough to quarantine the entire Federation was, again, not an issue for me to embarrass them with. Estonia, my Russian reading, and the Trans-Siberian journey had worn away the culture-shock she was hinting at. So I said it was the way they drive. 'They are CRAZY here!' I said and it was met with laughter. 'Crazy! Crazy! Crazy!' They could hardly control themselves and I had an answer I would always use.

At 1h20 a bell rang and the class pled that I return after lunch. Marina entered, said there were other plans for me and I was needed downstairs. Every woman had to have a picture taken with me. They fought over who got to sit where and which shoulders my arms were around. The teachers, other students and old people out walking—even the goddamn fire department—all had to see what the fuss was about. It was me, being the first native English speaker ever on the Institute grounds.

Marina pulled me away and introduced me to Mikhail, the regional arts/culture/foreigner-orientation guide. He ran us down the main street to the Stara Oscal museum and summoned a tour guide. The guide walked us around small fortress models, Tatar/Mongol/Polish-Lithuanian regalia seized by the Russians, and a 19th century house replete with a spinning wheel/ 'Red Corner' (where the icons sit), and a brick stove. I left with a small translated brochure as a keepsake from the museum staff.

Mikhail drove us around the city, NE, N, NW, E, SE, S, SW, W (as the districts were innovatively named). Stara Oscal is nationally credited for its cleanliness and green space. November still had left a little greenery and old women with twig brooms swept whatever fell from the trees. Apartment blocks sat fat everywhere. And in the old Russian home and dacha areas, gas was fed to them by an eight foot high pipeline that ran between them and the roads. There were cattle, geese, chickens, goats, and people everywhere.

Mikhail drove to the war memorial which housed remains of the soldiers from the last world war. 'People still look for the identification cards of loved ones in the forests', Marina translated. She said the cards were the Russian equivalent to metal 'dog tags' used by American soldiers but paper sadly doesn't last as long.

Mikhail eagerly decided he was going to drive us to a place no foreigner had been, except a few scientists. Until recently, it was a 'forbidden zone'. We wove through the industrial complexes, metallurgy buildings, refinery depots and concrete manufacturers. Then we edged up to a lookout and left the car. At the railing, I grew dizzy. It was the second largest open pit mine in Russia. Mikhail said the equivalent to 37 Giza pyramids of iron-ore had been extracted from the ground. And it was in progress. Dump trucks, with 12 foot wheels, were descending and ascending steep grades, in dark earth. There were excavators with room-sized shovels scraping deeper. Trains were constantly shuffling on the tracks, rearranging themselves around the main plant. From inside, a pressurized system fired the iron-ore via pipeline to *Gordenvy*, a city 20 kilometres away. (The Soviets planned that the two cities would be one merged city but there was still 20 kilometres of birch forest in the way). The view was overwhelming; an inverted mountain, a man-made crater visible from space. My camera couldn't take it all in.

We made our way back to town. The local market had every product imaginable on sale. I asked how markets functioned in the Soviet times, when such abundance was unheard of. Marina said there were times when very little was on the shelves for sale. 'Often the market was just a long line for nothing.' The market I saw was well-stocked with commodities and the queues were so short that there was no wonder that capitalism was beating out communism in a triumphant thunderclap. I should think that returning to the old ways could never happen. No one could stand it. They must, I concluded, wonder how they ever did. Everything in rural Stara Oscal was ten to twenty percent cheaper than in Voronezh.

We drove around an area that housed a group of fancy red brick homes belonging to the plant owners and industry managers. We drove by buildings that seemed iced together like gingerbread.

'In Gorbechev times,' Mikhail told me, '... it was said that by the year 2000, every Russian family would have an apartment'.

'And...' I prompted him, 'How far off were they?'

He and Marina laughed, 'Much... much off.' It was under *perestroika* that these apartments were built. One out of every ten workers came here and helped build these while the other nine people at the factory shared the workload of the tenth'. Russia gleamed for awhile. But then 'the crisis!' (as they prefer to call the Soviet collapse) happened.

Mikhail showed us the high-speed tram system that shuttled 15,000 workers a day to the smelter. He said that the tram drivers had been caught taking the tiny electric trains up to 180 km/h so the local Duma took out the 4th and 5th gears.

Mikhail drove us back to the Institute. A spectacular lunch had been planned in the director's office. We spoke about Russia, the effect of the collapse on the country, and economic recovery in the province. And we talked about those damn Russian hockey players who leave Russia and never come back. As we finished a half box of award-winning Russian choco-lates, the TV crew asked for another interview since I'd now seen the city. I avoided the strip-mining, spoke of how wonder-fully clean and green, the city was and tantalized them with how gifted I felt the students were. Since I was now familiar with the gradient of learning, I could tell that the students were headed for fluency. They had a passion for English as though it was the key to understanding themselves and their world. They saw a richer life if any of them could make it out of Stara Oscol and then Russia.

In the staff room, a math teacher flipped through a dictio-nary then fragmented out the sentence, 'Why you come to Russia?'

'To see you do that,' I answered.

I was on my knees scrubbing my Levi's inch by inch in the bathtub as water seeped into the hall rug and started up the wall carpets. The underwear, the socks, the pleated shirts, everything was washed and rinsed in safe, cold water. After I'd drained the tepid pool of murky residue, it all had to hang to dry. There were 34 points in my apartment where items could be left to dry; however guests are encouraged to stay away for the better part of two days after I do laundry. It is not uncommon for people to find my boxer shorts on the fridge, held up by my magnetic Roman alphabet. Or they may discover three different socks a floor below if the wind turns. Never take a washing machine or dryer for granted.

I dropped my film off at a small camera shop near my flat. I was told the pictures would be ready in the last half of the day. When I went in to pick them up, I paid and received a small envelope that could not have contained pictures. Inside the envelope were my negatives. This woman is nuts, I thought. I excused myself from the line with a puzzled look. I spotted a light table with eager people sliding their negatives around. The average Russian cannot afford to develop an entire roll of film and consequently they just have those they choose from the light table processed. I concluded that the best of Russian photography is in a drawer somewhere, undeveloped.

Nona's grandfather is a beekeeper. She asked me if I'd like any honey. Since I was using plentiful dollops of it in my tea, I handed her a hundred rubles. Two days later she came to class with a four gallon jar. I instantly felt badly that she'd had to transport it; buses and what-not. It was heavy and awkward. I accidentally nearly rolled it into traffic getting it home. But it was very good honey, the kind of good honey that stories are made of.

I began taking Italian lessons from Lucia. She had tried to round up a number of people to join but few wanted to invest their time in Italian. She only persuaded one young teacher named Ira to join. Ira taught economics at the Institute. Early one Saturday morning, Lucia and Ira came to my door and we started our class.

Lucia had obtained permission to make photocopies of course work (Sasha does not part with toner easily; it'd be easier to convince him you want to borrow his wife) and she spread them out. It was difficult for me to learn Italian with Lucia because she had to explain everything to me in French. When that didn't work, Ira tried to explain it in broken English. When that failed, I was stuck with an Italian-English dictionary. When that failed I made chai, which never fails.

Natasha introduced me to her link with a vodka factory. She knew the owner and I'd like to think they met while burning American dollar bills at the *Otlichniki Zona*. That was Natasha: mysterious, mystifying, mafia. One morning she organized a small tour that was a message to me that she had contacts. I was surprised when a driver for the distillery picked us up in a sleek black Volga and drove us across the frozen river to the Left Bank. Once there, we negotiated many side streets before finally pulling up to a rusty gate. An armed guard checked our credentials and wheezed the corroded iron door open.

We met Viktor, the manager, an inspiring man worshipped by many a Russian. As he stood beside us pointing out buildings, his cell phone rang. It was cold and draughty in the compound but Viktor made no apologies for his phone call. If you are important enough to have a cell phone then any call is important. In the yard where Natasha and I stood, there was a long white Cadillac, the only one in Voronezh. Along another wall was a 1950 Zhul stretch limo that had been used during Brezhnev's time to carry Party officials. Viktor closed his phone and swiveled to us. Natasha translated his explanation, 'Business in Voronezh is business.'

Viktor escorted us inside to an enormous room where the bottles were being cleaned. It was staffed by two women who looked completely bored with the whole process. We moved to another room where a line of vats stood slowly fermenting critical ingredients. Viktor had a particular fondness for the temperature control and he slid the lever back and forth many times.

The final room was where the bottling took place. A dozen people with white headscarves diligently worked their individual part of the line. There were machines that spun the bottles around and machines that sealed them with a cap. Then the bottles rolled along a little path of rollers to the machine that pasted on the label. Just as we entered, there was shouting and Russian pejoratives. The label machine had decided against labeling and flung labels into the air. Viktor hollered in quick Russian and two men leapt at the labeling machine with screwdrivers.

There was a room dedicated to the lineage of the vodka factory. There were trophy shelves with old bottles with old labels. On the wall were pictures of staff from various eras. There were photographs of vat upgrades, new plumbing and the installation of the label machine currently giving the men with screwdrivers trouble.

Natasha told me that none of the vodka I'd seen was for Voronezh. It was all bound for Moscow. In fact, it was illegal for anyone to consume *this* vodka in the province of Voronezh. Viktor was again engaged on his phone as we left and could only wave goodbye. Viktor continued to talk while taking two gift bottles of vodka from the trophy shelf. He handed them to me and winked.

Sergei continued to improve. As his English progressed, he was able to convey to me more about his life, more about his family and more about his ambitions. I learned to filter out what he was saying and focus on what he was saying wrong. Sergei had many faults in his English and when I pointed them out, he would swear in prolific Russian. Da, he would say. And he would try harder. When you are trying to grasp every nuance of a new language, recurring errors are frustrating. At times Sergei would stand up and walk around the room trying to plant the concept. He was aware that I wasn't enjoying his cassette tapes. They were boring and flat.

Still, I was being paid enough per hour from Sergei to listen to them. I met few people who could afford what Sergei was paying me. He earned a good wage as a programmer and his wife was a math teacher so he had the means to fund his language study. But those damn American tapes were a sad substitute for a teacher.

Sasha, my immediate boss, left for America. I went to the train station to see him off. On the frosty platform, we shivered waiting for the school's director, Mr. Zolotovinski. Sasha was wearing his yellow suit. We smoked and told international jokes to each other. I told him about American women and gave him a few pick-up lines to try out. Mr. Zolotovinski approached us on the platform. Being that he is an honourable person commanding profound respect, I had learned the phrase *'uva-zhae-mye gas-podean pryezi-dent'* meaning 'I greet you, you honourable person commanding profound respect'. He was visibly pleased and returned fire with something I couldn't even be sure was Russian. They boarded their carriage and departed for Moscow, and then…that place of dreams, *America*.

It was Sasha's first trip 'outside' and he was ecstatic, even though he had an eleven hour train ride to endure to Moscow, then transit to the airport, and four hours of waiting in the gulag that is Moscow's Sheremetyevo Airport. I saw the anticipation and angst in my friend who was going to discover something he pictured as the greener side of the fence. Whether he was capable of translating the two week visit, I did not know. But he would be on American soil before anyone found out.

One day in the office, Marina produced a videocassette.

'I have a video of you' said Marina.

'I was young, I needed the money.'

'What?' she said vacantly.

'What-what'.

'Something tells me you aren't handling the local radiation levels well… this is your interview from Stara Oscal.' She said it with a bit of dismay. Marina was dejected. The television people had completely edited her translating out and thus eliminated her from the taping.

'Oh… I'm still in it though, right? Otherwise it'd seem pointless'

When I got home, I checked all the cables on the VCR and let a whirring stop. Then carefully I placed the cassette into the machine, slowly snapped the lid shut and pressed play.

The news item was professional. I was proud of myself. I did feel sorry that they cut Marina's translating work, which she had done so well, but if I may say so, she was so professionally cut that you couldn't tell she'd even been in the vicinity.

That night I was awakened by an electronic noise in the living room. It usually takes a smash, sneeze, or footsteps to get me out of bed and so I just waited. I listened to a drone, then a stressed grinding. The noise stopped. I could hear several clicks and I knew at once that it was the VCR doing something it had not been programmed for. It was eating the interview. By the time I had found the VCR in the dark, it was too late. The entire tape was destroyed. It had been on loan to me and the institute wanted the copy to place in their collection of school effects. I tried to think of excuses but realized the truth may be the only thing they'd believe.

During one class, I circulated an article from an American Business magazine. The editorial described the current 'life' in Russia as being prosperous, exciting and vibrant with the 'new' market economy situation. In my first few days in the city, I had been told many times that 'Voronezh is not Moscow'. To the outside world, Moscow was the barometer for the collective economic health of Russia. However, to the rest of the country, Moscow was an entity all its own and it didn't speak at all for the land and lives outside its city limits. I spoke candidly with the students about what I saw in Voronezh and, on a larger scale, Russia, and therefore why I thought the article was misleading, I said:

"Under gun barrel grey skies, the city is filled with concrete buildings of the same dim relentless hue. The roads are unkempt, some are even impassable. Trash is abundant. People stand for twelve hours selling anything they own or can produce. One man is in the same place everyday selling shoe inserts hand-cut from a worn rug. A woman sells sunflower seeds she's grown herself at her dacha. Another begs, weeping behind an icon, for kopecks. Packs of mangy stray dogs run through the streets, upending garbage cans and threatening babushkas. Many of the Gypsy children roaming about are looking for a chance to steal a wallet or purse. Sidewalks are closer to mountain bike trails and rubble is recklessly strewn on the footpaths. Only half the streetlights work. Condemnable buildings are occupied. The antiquated transit system services every part of town with choking diesel buses, 1960s trolleys and a tram system that has pressed worn tracks beneath the dirt. Many of the cars are vintage Volgas and barely-running Ladas but every now and then a BMW 535i or a Toyota 4Runner with tinted windows barrels by...."

The class told me how they saw things:

'Every business is illegal,' said Mikhail who faces conscription into the army. He was bound for Chechnya 'to die... I will *die* there'. He continued, 'There is no honest way to earn big money. It is corrupt, Russia is just a pyramid of corruption.'

Nona spoke. 'If you want to start a business, you can't get a loan. So you go to the mafia. Every business pays the mafia... every single one. If you don't pay them, they will blow up your business. If you get too big, they will kill you and take the business.'

Another, usually timid student, Angelika, looked at me, and said, 'Businesses pay both the police and the mafia to survive.' And she gave an example of police corruption, 'An illegal kiosk sells vodka. It doesn't pay taxes but instead the police wait and fine the people who buy the vodka.'

'If you have big money, you have big problems. It is easier to be poor,' said Kendra.

Alexei was reading the magazine and contributed, 'I wish *this* situation was real! Hah! I guess Americans are thinking we are doing *all* right now.'

'The police will stop people peddling apples or seeds that they grew at their dacha and demand money. If the sellers don't have any, the police tell them to go home because they aren't paying taxes,' said Anastasia, 'The police are the second mafia.'

I asked about the wages. The women who sell seeds make 50 rubles a day, less than two American dollars for 12 hours standing. Alexei again: 'No one wants to clean up the streets. No one wants to fix the railings or pick up the garbage. Russian people are tolerant. Too tolerant, too afraid to speak out or clean up. It won't get better here. I think it is impossible.'

The whole class understood my impressions and no one defended the fact that the country is not a very good place for most of the population. The students all felt that they were beneath an umbrella of corruption and would never lead the lives they used to dream of living. Kendra said she didn't dream anymore, 'When I was a child – yes, but not anymore.'

They weren't necessarily envious of the New Russians, the Oligarchs, the fortunate ones to be riding the wave of a new system, but Mikhail ended the class by passing on a Russian proverb: It is not a problem my cow is dead; it is a problem my neighbour has a live one.

. . .

When I entered the office one morning, all three occupants swiveled their chairs around. Marina was white. She was about to tell me something I would not like.

'Brant… this came for you,' she said. She unfolded a small sheet of paper. I took it and read my way through the Russian. It was my bill for the internet. I moved my finger along the columns and looked for the highest figure. The bill was 5800 rubles. I did the familiar conversion and arrived at $200 American. I turned as white as Marina. This amount was more than she earned in eight months. It was a month's pay for me. For this sum I could have taken the whole office to Moscow, created a political party or started my own Cyrillic ninja school. I scratched out some numbers on a scrap piece of paper and discovered roughly 120 hours of usage were billed. I then tallied what I felt I was using: three hours a night, four or five nights a week, carry the two. I was short 40+ hours but, as I told Marina, it was in the ballpark. Then I explained what 'in the ballpark' meant.

'Well…' Marina said, 'What are you going to do?'

'… what would Jesus do?' I said.

'Do you really think that is relevant?'

'No it just popped into my head. But while we're on the topic, I'd like to think he'd send that fat IP guy to hell with an Arabic version of Windows 95.'

'Russians live in reality, I'd like you to visit it for a few moments so we can deal with this.'

I paid the amount and swore to keep better track of my hours. One night as I was inspecting my computer's settings, I found a checkmark in a box I hadn't noticed before. My computer was set to dial someplace in Sweden where lonely stewardesses chat at 1am every night. Therein lay the problem;

a renegade check. My bill did come down but it was many, many rubles from what a Russian considered decent.

Anya's other grandmother lives on the Left Bank and had a lighting fixture that had ceased to work. Since I had a rudimentary knowledge of electrical matters, Anya asked if I would repair the item in exchange for lunch. I took a trolleybus through the outer districts and crossed the river on its south bridge. Anya was waiting at the bus stop. I got off and greeted her in a surrounding of identical apartments.

We walked, breaking fresh snow through old snow and made it to the tenth storey flat. Babushka was overjoyed to see me. She ran around tightening bed sheets and sweeping doormats. She spoke softly and looked at me through tired eyes. Babushka had lived in the same apartment for 55 years. The view out the window was of similar apartment blocks and terribly bleak.

Babushka and Anya created lunch while I acquainted myself with the ceiling light. The problem involved a minor cleaning of the worn contacts. When I had finished and the moment came to turn on the light, I thought I'd earned salvation. Babushka fidgeted with her knuckles and said *spacebo* many times. The light hadn't worked for two years. We ate humble Russian dumplings and Babushka pressed me to marry Anya. Anya looked ready to comply.

I sat in the tiny flat and listened to Babushka's stories. She lost her husband 35 years before and had spent the time, as many Russian widows do, shut away from the world. Babushka recounted the war years, the losing of her soldier son and the dreary life that ensued. She was a Russian archetype.

. . .

I discovered a bank just doors down from me on a backstreet. There was always an armed guard or two at the entrance. Inside it was a mesh of marble and glass. It was beautiful but in Russian tradition, it was agonizingly slow. The third time I went, the armed guard outside stopped me. Was I selling American money? Before I had a proper plan, I'd already said yes, fifty dollars worth in three bills, two denominations... I spend a lot of my life dealing with consequences. Would I sell it to him? I would get more from him than the bank, he said. We casually walked to his small Lada. As he entered the car, twice he caught his semi-automatic rifle in the door. I pulled out my wad and hid it again. Holding his hands beneath the worn steering wheel, the guard counted off 1500 black market rubles.

We both peered out the fogged up windows and then stealthily swapped the currencies. For months, I kept coming back and he kept buying. His name was Vlad and he was blind in one eye.

Disaster struck one night. I was going through my usual routine of making chai before bed. I picked up the box of matches and chose one with a medium-sized sulphur head. I turned the gas on and skillfully moved my hand to the area near the whistling jets. I began to panic; this is normal. When the stove ignited, I reached for my old Russian tea kettle. I turned on the faucet but there was no water, just a gulping sound. I turned off the stove and went to bed without my tea.

At some time during the night the water came back on. I was asleep and did not hear it flowing with great pressure into my little Russian sink. The water carried up to the edge of the counter and spent the next few hours draining through the floor, into the stereo store. The damage was minimal to substantial depending on who you asked. I had to pay what amounted to a month's salary and promise to be more careful. A cup of tea would never be the same.

I bet Marina ten rubles Sasha would not return from the States. 'Russia produces the best defectors in the world,' I said confidently. I was sure he was gone, working at a cheap 2-for-1 pizza place in Nebraska, then I spotted his yellow suit coming down the sidewalk. I didn't have to pay Marina because I had bet another ten rubles that if he did return, he'd be wearing that specific suit. Sasha entered the office area a new man. As an interpreter, he had translated meetings for the big guys. He had entertained dignitaries, translated speeches, and 'shopped' at the local 7-11 until two a.m. when they kicked him out. His every free second in Virginia was spent 'shopping'. He passed his photos around the office. Most of his pictures were of supermarkets, strip malls and quizzical clerks.

I don't drink alcohol well. For years I did. I drank, joyfully, gratuitously, and lots. I partied with people, I partied alone. I enjoyed drinking. But I could see problems manifesting. At a hazy point in our relationship that I don't really remember, drinking had become an unwanted dependency, a crutch, an elephant in the living room, a proverbial car in the ditch. Alcohol became synonymous with bad luck. I vowed on my thirtieth birthday to do away with alcohol and cigarettes. With wheezing lungs and a pounding head, I surrendered. That was two years ago. I could no longer drink. I knew it to be true. I knew, too, that placing myself in Russia was placing myself at risk. In November, at the picnic in the forest, I had consumed more than enough vodka to remind me why I had stopped drinking. Of course that point only presented itself when I had reached the limit and then overshot it like the party missile I had once been. I made myself new promises and stayed away from alcohol. Through autumn I was rarely tempted. In one class at the university, the end of the school's semester was celebrated with a lot of beer. I abstained, even with the beautiful women tempting me, coaxing me to enjoy myself, to take off my tie, to live, to drink. I was strong and did not fall off the *vasitchka*. But days later, without giving much thought to it, I stopped by a small kiosk and bought two bottles of vodka. I walked home with an already fuzzy grip on reality. I was never a drinker of hard liquor but vodka was the drink of choice in Russia and buying anything else was against the ghosts of tradition. If I was going to drink - and I was - I was going to do it in the customs of my new country. Clanking my way up my staircase, I withdrew my keys and entered my room for the last sober time in a while.

I was well into my first bottle of vodka when the feeling came over me that I just may be doing something stupid. I carried on, however, with a positivism that everything was fucking awesome and I should just enjoy it. My music was loud. A bootleg copy of Sarah Brightman cycled. I redecorated, cleaned the toilet, and wrote unintelligible letters home. I hit the chandelier and spent an hour trying to put the crystals back. And I wasn't drinking alone, oh no, I was drinking *with* Russia. I was feeling an elation, a stupefying hilarity all Russians feel when they drink vodka. Well maybe not. My purpose was not social; I was bent on getting drunk. And what little humour, comfort, and solace I was to enjoy lasted about four minutes. The first bottle was finished and rolled away as I cracked the seal on the second. It was at this point in my stupor that I threw on my winter clothes and challenged four lanes of trams and traffic to the kiosks for some local music. I bought nine CDs, two nail clippers, and a Russian Playboy with Marilyn Monroe on the cover.

With the second bottle lying drained on its side, I turned to the souvenir bottles of vodka from the distillery tour. They were staring at me. I couldn't go after them, they were illegal and they were gifts right from the distillery. As I ripped the safety seal off the first, I envisioned myself in Anya's babushka's apartment, unscrewing another vodka bottle twenty years later and wondering if my pension cheque was in the mailbox. I put the last of my energy into writing a poem about Anya's poor babushka.

> Heavy feet walk over the trail
> Poised in the steps of another
> Iron pokes from the snow in some
> Fashioning of a swing set
> But the head does not lift
> to see the children play
> Oh you old frail babushka
> Last you looked; last you knew
> You too were here in an autumn sweep
> Youth upon you and a son on the swing
> With laughter between you
> Now he has gone to war and he is here no more
> And the woman at the swing bears
> No memory to you
> For the room will be cold
> And that is what you look at
> In your late days,
> The last of things to dread
> Weariness is eating your grip
> On the sack of soup onions and milk

Curses swirl from your warm breath
Into a sky that saps it of meaning
Never could you know the child
On the swing
Not again, not ever again,
For the room will be cold
… the room will be cold

I stared out the window at the snowy day and the people dashing to and fro. I stared for a long time. Russia, my Russia, was outside my windows. My Ladas, my fur stoles, my Rossiya department store, my Russian smog. I had a glass, a worn Russian tumbler that came with the apartment, and I kept filling it up. I realized then I was depressed. I suffer from regular cycles of depression and this one challenged my ability to abstain from drinking. My guard had been down. Oh well, I chimed, plenty of vodka to cure all that….

I drank far too much vodka. I was in a state of mind and body just short of requiring hospitalization and a five-point harness. I was lying on the bed convinced if I was still and kept a shallow breath that I would make it through the night and no one would know.

Marina had a key to my apartment and let herself in when I did not answer the door.

'How are you feeling?' she asked cautiously.

'I am one long inch away from happiness…'

'That's the cost of the curse,' she said, using her toe to move a vodka bottle across the floor. 'I'm sure the devil loves the attention.'

'I didn't mean to get to this point, I was just walking by the…'

'No explanations please. It keeps you interesting,' she said.

Marina seated herself on the bow on my bed. 'Besides... you have nothing to hide and nowhere to hide it.'

'I figured that drinking wasn't a perfect science. I was wrong,' I said.

'Is that a reason or an excuse?'

'It's sort of an enlightenment...'

'Is there something I could do to make you feel better?'

'Sex,' I answered in italics.

'Sex is psychology and friction.' She put her chin confidently on her fist. 'Neither of which I want to share with you.'

'You aren't *fond* of me?' I said.

'As a friend, I am. Beyond that I find you a turn-off.'

'What does that mean?'

'It's the difference between a blink and a wink,' she said and then she blinked.

I rolled my face into my pillow. 'Vodka has made me a statistic. God has allowed me to be an example. I depart a martyr of excess... and deprived of a final bonk too.'

'What are you saying?'

'I'm going towards the light... don't try to stop me.'

'You are not going to die,' she said.

'I'm taking my soul back to the manufacturer to get Brant 2.0'

'You are not going to die.'

'You can be so sure?' I said mimicking her accent.

'There is a Russian proverb-'

'Oh there *always* is isn't there...'

'You won't drown if your fate is to be shot.'

I was angry and upset with the situation. First, I'd been found out, and second, I was out of vodka. I felt like I was two miles behind the parade. I laid there on my lumpy bed and Marina sat beside me. I felt despicable. I had my trademark migraine. I knew that the full hang-over was mere hours away and at that point depression and migraine would collide creating the grizzliest of human suffering. I call it a Category Five. I was not happy with the forecast. Marina started stroking my hair. She knew I felt horrible; there is an empathy in Russia. She knew I was going to feel worse as the last of the vodka wore off. She counted something on her fingers and decided she could help somehow. Marina phoned her mother, a nurse, and was given a number to call. She called and placed a kind of order. Marina entered my room and told me to wait, soon everything would get better.

There was a horrible screech from the doorbell that made my scrotum crawl. Marina answered it. There were two equally unattractive nurses and they entered my room. They were dressed in white with white hats and each carried a weathered satchel. Marina explained they were going to administer drugs to help me withdraw from the alcohol I had ingested. The two women pricked me in different spots and warm fluids slid into my veins. I looked up at the nearest nurse. She smiled. Her teeth looked like Stonehenge. I had a rush of trauma, a feeling of panic, and finally some anxiety. I didn't know what they were giving me and I had, somewhere, my own imported needles for just such an occasion. As I started getting excited, a hush came over me. I felt worse and better at the same time. The nurses left the room and spoke to Marina for a few moments. I began to get sleepy and pulled my comforter up to my neck. Dusk had fallen and a single bulb cast the shadows of Marina and the nurses on my pale wall. Tomorrow, I told myself, everything would be alright. Marina came in and stroked my hair and told me the medications would help me get over my 'bout'. I thanked her, asked her to thank her mom, and then thanked her again. She left. I could hear the door shut quietly. I could hear the traffic fighting the snow outside. I could hear my own heart. Yes, everything was going to be okay.

I felt something hovering over me. When I opened my eyes, there were four aliens looking down. My first inclination was to fight my way out of my bed and run outside with flailing arms. No, I decided, that wouldn't be prudent. I stared at the beings and slowly sat up. The aliens looked like noses; it's hard to describe. There were aliens around my entire room. There were aliens by the ironing board and aliens in the living room; in the hallway and in the kitchen. There were aliens everywhere in my flat. I had completely flipped. My movie was over. The initial four beings communicated through telepathy and told me I hadn't flipped, which I found somewhat comforting though not altogether reassuring. They were allergic to light one of them said and they asked me to keep the lights off. And would I refrain from smoking? They said it was illegal in the future. I was absolutely sure that I had gone crazy, that I would be lucky to escape from Russia before anyone noticed I had driven across the state line in my brain. I told them I would open the window but smoking was non-negotiable.

The beings claimed to be from the future. They had travelled .69768 of a parsec through what we call Cygnus-X, the land of the black hole. I noted all of this down on my computer. My 'visit' continued for hours, eight in fact. I taught them to play chess; they taught me to read minds. I traded an American ten dollar bill for 6 dofgors which later ran away. I gave them a stamp of Sputnik. They gave me a fullhern. It also ran away. I showed them how to do Rubik's Cube. They got hooked on my imported mango juice.

I showed them the internet, a concept they were familiar with but not the content. We surfed everything from commercial aviation, war archives, and the Vatican to forests, gold reserves, and naked pictures of Angelica Huston. They were a little impatient with my dial-up modem but I reminded them that it was *they* who had landed in Russia. We exchanged ideas, played with the future of the NHL, and solved pi.

When daylight appeared and drew great lines through my rooms, the aliens hid in the shadows. They hated my cheap Russian cigarettes; this was because cheap Russian cigarettes smell horrible to everyone and the aliens were essentially big noses. As the sun rose over the Rossiya and cascaded through my thin cotton drapery, they confided they could stay no longer, the light and the smoke was far too much for them to handle. I felt as if I'd done the entire planet a huge injustice. I wanted to apologize but suddenly the door shot open with so much force that it left an imprint on the wall carpet. One by one they slinked off. If they'd left their spaceship outside and unattended, it was likely stolen for scrap by resident babushkas.

I did feel better the next day. I was certain that the entire alien session was an accident but what had caused it? All those hours with creatures from the future... it felt so real! They knew things about me I had forgotten. Combinations to locks I no longer own. Phone numbers of people who no longer have phones. What did I experience during those hours? I called Marina at once. She didn't feel too comfortable when I explained what had transpired since she'd left.

'Aliens?' she asked. 'As in-'

'No, I don't mean a bunch of foreign ESL teachers....'

This set things in motion rather quickly. As soon as Marina understood what I'd been through, she called the nurses and two doctors to find an answer. It was found that I had been administered two drugs which weren't compatible. It seems the nurses had screwed up and drugged me with a concoction that no carbon-based Canadian should be drugged with. Everyone else involved in this localized incident seemed relieved there was now a medical conclusion to this story. I still believed whole-heartedly that I had seen aliens. And not just one or two but several and not just for a blink of an eye but throughout the night.

Marina never mentioned the incident again and I did not tell anyone about it for months. When I emailed a friend back home he laughed and said he was something of an authority on these matters. My experience was not familiar to him. He was sure that it'd been the medication, a botched case of detoxifying a drunk.

'Cygnus X is a Black Hole… they'd never make it here. Trust me,' he said.

'Black body thermo-radiation engines with over-clocked tachyonistic fuel cores…' I replied.

'Plausible, highly doubtful. That shit's hard to come by.'

I told him I could read minds but that the minds around me were thinking in Russian which posed a problem. If I was hearing voices, he said, then there were other issues I needed to address. I would like to think what occurred that night was real. I mean it's a hell of a story. And they forgot their probe.

I focused on healing myself back for the onslaught of winter. The days grew shorter as more hours of daylight were lost. In Russia, autumn succumbs to an immediate Arctic front, dying colourfully as winter ascends. I was spending my nights indoors and watching the populace waddle around in their thick clothing.

With Christmas and New Years about to happen, I found myself pleased with my autumn. I had become a teacher. And through my teaching I learnt far more than I had taught. I had confidence I'd never felt before. My teaching supplies were spent. I had brought things that I didn't use and there were many things I should have brought more of. There were thoughts of things I'd never known and thoughts that I'd done away with. I felt Russian and part of a big picture. With that, autumn cooled off allowing winter to cover nature in the posterity of a snowfall. The snow was as welcome as the hoarfrost. The icicles were as welcome as the cold temperature. This was a part of my dream - to see Russia in her most famous of seasons.

Russia is winter. The country, for all its magnitude, is pretty much the frozen quadrant of the globe. I would often go walking at night just to experience the extent of the cold. Layering myself, double-scarfing my neck, I would chart out a small square in which to wander. There were a few factory smokestacks that were exhausting heat. In the exceptional cold, the smoke was buoyant, turning to trails like separating cotton balls. The haphazard apartment blocks became cozy and welcoming against the night and the cold. They rose up in softly-lit elevations that hid their manufacturing scars.

In the freezing air, I would walk hoping to gain body heat and sense of place. When Russians dress for the cold, they dress for every potential event relating to temperature change. It may happen that –5 turns to –25 in the space of half a minute so it is wise to wear all the clothing that may be needed. Anya layered such that she looked double her weight. I accidentally pointed that out once. Many of the women on the street had gone to great lengths to try to look good in spite of their substantial clothing. Few succeeded. When Russians are dressed for winter, the sidewalks, buses, and stores shrink.

Sometimes I forgot where I was. Days passed without any fondness of living *in* Russia. There were those days when hammers and sickles didn't jump at me as being iconic gems of an empire; a mess of heads and fur hats didn't phase me as foreign; when the jockeying of trams and traffic I so loved was missed while mundanely watching for the cracked green light to walk. Some days were just as much work, just as frustrating, just as routine as a day back home. Wake up, attempt a shower, work, sleep. Yes sometimes the novelty just wore off. I always remembered to tip my hat to Lenin in his square; simply a must. Sometimes his stern appearance was striking, causing me to remember to 'live' in the moment, to see myself in the present tense. Sometimes I felt like a trespasser in his ideology; other times I'm sure he knew my ilk, under these circumstances, was coming sometime in the Soviet Union's future.

Late one night Anya and I went for a walk. There were starry skies and a temperature of sixteen degrees below zero. Anya was wearing a full-length mink coat and a leather cap. A half a foot of fresh snow had fallen. I had taken these trails before through the cookie-cutter apartment blocks and the communal squares of debris. Often I was walking over icy puzzles of asphalt or braving snow flurries so I couldn't see the peculiar beauty of the winter scene. It took a Russian epiphany to put it right.

In a fresh moment's pause, Russia 'happened'. The snow did something it hadn't done in the weeks before. It shaded and contrasted. The bare sixty-watt bulbs in the tenements threw out golden panes of light. Cooled smoke spilt into the sky from factory stacks. Flakes fell about us, brushing our cheeks. I waited while Anya wrote her name in the snow. Other couples strolled arm in arm. Pushkin recited, Dostoevsky taunted, and

Tolstoy lived deep in the night's haunt of winter. I caught sight of a wooden house huffing smoke, with zigzags of firewood along its length. It was my own picture of the quintessential house in the woods…the vision spoke of all I'd dreamt of owning against a rural Wyoming hillside in years gone by. Here it was in Voronezh - a fire in the hearth, wood ash and cedar scent in the gusts. The walk was all I had imagined of Russia.

Most of Russia is aware that the balance of the Western world celebrates Christmas on the 25th of December. Many of them know that stockings are hung, halls are decked; and Saint Nicholas breaches property through chimneys early on that particular day. But Russians do, for the better part, treat December 25th like any other day. Russian holidays survive on the Julian calendar which, because it does not account for leap years, leaves its date of commencement subject to different days. Russia used the Julian calendar until 1918 then switched to the Gregorian calendar we Westerners use. However, the Russian Orthodox Church continues the Julian calendar approach. This makes celebrating the winter holidays in Russia a little confusing. In order to adjust for these differences, many Russians just celebrate the whole way through.

Lucia is the only other one concerned with December 25th. In Russia, I thought I'd be swapping happy Christmas stories, eggnog, and reindeer jokes. But *nyet*. The big day in Russia is New Year's Eve, the one celebrated on the 31st of December, when it appears as though they drink and enter a new paradigm of hope with delirium tremens. The Orthodox Christmas on January 7th is child-based and remains something reserved for young memories.

I spent my Christmas Eve with Anya, wrapped in a room full of candles. It was a quiet affair. I had a Boney M Christmas disc and it went around and around. My little Czech lights blinked and twinkled. There was much chai to drink and a special tart, bought from the Rossiya, to eat. In the heat of the festive moment I produced a small present for Anya. It was a present that would let her know my feelings, something that would tell her that I cared for and trusted her. She opened the little box. Inside was a key, the key for my flat. Her face went red and she shook with emotion. She knew the only reason I would be giving this to her was to tell her I was inching closer to a full-fledged though still covert relationship. These things take time. Anya hugged me with full strokes of my hair. I told her that it was for convenience, it didn't necessarily permit her in the flat any time that she wanted. I told her that Marina, for purely work-related purposes, had the only other copy.

I had a small pine branch to serve as my Christmas tree, one no more than a few inches in length. It beamed with the tail end of my Czech-made lights and told everyone on the street I was celebrating the Gregorian calendar. Christmas Eve was a sweet night that slowly left us sleepy on the couch in the front room. I carried Anya to the bedroom and there we slept until the rise of a foggy dawn.

I woke up wanting to peek at the strewn gifts. (I'd set them out the night before, ever-so-quietly so I could play both Santa and maniacal child myself.) Anya, though her means were modest, had been able to afford a stylish amber picture which I immediately cherished. I hung it on the wall beside my Tatu band poster and I could tell she took this as a special gesture because her eyes welled with tears. Nothing until then had flanked the Tatu band poster.

We had a full breakfast which Anya had prepared out of only two or three ingredients. She was amazingly versatile when it comes to food. I ate my meal in large pieces and went to bathe. I had adjusted to the water and gas mechanics. I seldom filled the room with gas and I survived times when the water ran cold without wanting to pack up and go home.

The weather was horrible. It was a few measly degrees above zero and the streets were melting themselves into icy pools that stretched entire blocks. Anya and I marched along back roads to the train station. Anya, topped with a black beret, watched as her train slowly docked at the berth and extended its steps. I thanked her for making my Christmas special. She kissed me back and smiled a smile only she could do, for it involved a little shake. It was a smile made for goodbyes.

The train eased off its brakes and started rolling by. I couldn't find Anya in the windows so I just waved to everyone, mouthing 'Merry Gregorian Christmas'. When the final car had left the station I walked down Prospect Revolution on my way home. Bookstores seem to grab me by the collar when I walk by them and I left the final establishment with four Christmas gifts to myself. Yet, it did not appear to be Christmas out. There wasn't any change in the number of people hustling through the stores and the temperature remained pathetic; quite unprofessional for a winter holiday. I browsed through a pipe store with pipes, tobacco, and accessories far beyond my price range. As I walked by Lenin's Square, there were workmen trying to hoist the massive tree that would signal the New Year to the city. I smiled and tipped my hat to Lenin. 'Merry Christmas Vlad.'

A few friends arrived in the afternoon and brought with them small gifts. Lucia and Natasha came, quite startling to me, at the same time.

'Whew, thank God Anya's gone… I don't *do* awkward very well'

Marina, Elena, and Oleg appeared soon after. Once everyone had their tea, I peeled back the paper on the gifts. I received a copy of Bach's *Well Tempered Clavier* from Natasha, a piece she knew I'd searched the whole city for. It was accompanied by a rare edition of an Italian Opera disc. She also gave me Leo Tolstoy's *Chem Lyudi Zhevye* (How People Live) in Russian. She had spent an undisclosed amount of organized crime money on me and for her I had an unwrapped Russian copy of Richard Bach's *Jonathon Livingston Seagull*.

The secretary Elena gave me a gift set of Vanilla cigars. For her I had an unwrapped Russian copy of Richard Bach's *Jonathon Livingston Seagull*.

From Oleg, the gentleman who works at the Duma in Moscow (he resides in Voronezh sometimes), I received a CD of Zhirinovsky singing, and an authentic shirt from the Russian Navy. For him I had an unwrapped Russian copy of Richard Bach's *Jonathon Livingston Seagull*.

Marina, knowing that my true purpose in life is driving, gave me a road atlas of Russia. For her I had an unwrapped Russian copy of Richard Bach's *Jonathon Livingston Seagull*.

So much for awkward, I thought, this is almost embarrassing…

'Oh!' I interjected myself, 'Here, these go with the books…' I went to a drawer and pulled out a few small pieces of stiff paper, each one with the face of the first few Communists. 'They're BookMarx!' I said, 'Marx, Engels, Lenin, Trotsky… here take one and pass them on.'

I was pleased with all of my gifts and I laid them out on my windowsill.

That night Sergei came over to pick me up. I had been invited to share Christmas dinner with his family. We took a taxi-bus and practiced his English on the ride. We climbed out at a stop and made our way through a forest of crumbling apartments. The snow that fell wasn't the kind of snow with flakes that rhymes with the season's spirit but rather a rain that fell somewhere between almost rain, almost hail. It made big slushy puddles of thick mud-brown water.

His wife Oxana had spared no expense to make the table alive with all sorts of coloured foods. Sergei had a sick passion for the Beatles. I have never met such a hardcore yet late-blooming Beatles fan as was he. Sergei, after introducing his young boy Pool, loaded the night's music on his computer and let it play.

'Pool, now that's a strange Russian name,' I said.

'Pool, after the Beatle. Pool McCartney,' replied Sergei.

Pool was nine or ten and ate everything on his plate like a true Russian. We had caviar. There was a plate of Friendship Cheese and gobs of salad. Oxana laid out a fatty piece of meat that looked like it had been chewed before. There were vegetables that looked like fruit and there was fruit that tasted like vegetables. The Bee-Gees played a song and then came the goddamn Beatles again. Russians are hip to listen to the music that spanned thirty years in the West. Remember, Western music hit Russia all at once. It is not uncommon to hear Metallica follow the theme from Titanic or Enya interrupted to play Jethro Tull. And of course there are times reserved for Russia's culture of opera, instrumental and choir. At Sergei's, there was singing, lip-synching and much eating.

I said goodbye to Sergei, Oxana, and Pool. They asked if I would like assistance in catching the bus. I smiled and said I would not only find it easily, I would call them in an hour to tell them I had made it home safe. Through the streets I roamed. I was soon lost. And I had 'Hey Jude' going around in my head which was more annoying than being lost. When I decided that I would return, laugh off my senselessness and ask for help, I couldn't tell Sergei's apartment from any other. The countless dark towers of his suburb were identical. And so I walked, urging myself onwards as I strode deeper and deeper into the suburbs of Voronezh. I tried twice to flag a car but was told I was too far out.

After an hour, I found a rather broad street with a group of people waiting for a bus. I joined them and boarded the 42A which took me three miles from my home. I partially walked this distance in defeat. And then came a small mini-van that I was familiar with: the *march-routka*. This concept should be implemented world-wide. These mini-buses, thirteen-passenger *Zhuls*, circle their routes, with or without people. If you see one, you flag it, and it follows its route. You tell the driver where to stop. These *march-routkas* buzz all over, every five, twenty or sixty minutes. If they're full, they pass you by.

The transportation in Voronezh goes like this:

Tram - it is the least 'fun' and it is reserved for old people and, said Anya, whores...trams cost 1 ruble 50 kopeks (12 cents). They cover a good part of the city. In a surprising agenda of infrastructure, there are bridges in Voronezh with trams running down the middle. They are cold and muddy for much of the year so trams were a last resort.

Trolleybuses - some trolleys are Swedish and they are a nice ride. But most aren't Swedish and aren't a nice ride. A lot of the city is covered with trolley routes. Voronezh is gridded in aerial webs of electricity for the trams and trolleybuses. The latter cost 2 rubles 50kopeks (18 cents).

Buses - they are everywhere. They carry 28 passengers at minimum. You can never see out the windows because it is either too crowded or the windows are dirty. The majority of the buses drive with the grill missing which exposes things like fans, belts and the drivers' feet. The cost is 3 rubles (24 cents). (Of note, every vehicle in Voronezh, be it a bus or a car, is a manual transmission.)

Marche-Routkas - this is a heck of a system as noted. It is cozy. There are curtains on the windows and the seats are nice after a day of walking, standing, or working. If I am in the back, I pass my money through three people so it gets to the front guy and they all in turn hand me back my receipt and change. This country is more open that way than any crowded elevator I've ever been in back home.

Flagging a car averages 30 rubles (~$1.00) to the places I go. It's usually the result of not being able to stand one more trip on a tram or trolleybus. Transportation is a social event and being packed into a confined space with people who are farting is a good reason to want a more personal touch. And so I flag a car. Some people, I've been told, go missing after flagging cars. Where they go, I do not know. But I bet it's cold there.

Dear Diary, December 31st

It is seven o'clock New Years Eve. The flat is swept. The termites are fenced off like a Parisian football match. The rug has been beaten and flipped over. I've sponged down the counters and other things that used to be shiny. There were three sponges. I relegated each to a place i.e. toilet, kitchen sink and bathtub. Then Lucia cleaned my coffee cup with one she should not have.

Had to buy a new sponge. And a new cup.

The last three days have been firework hell. It sounded as if there was a 'conflict' developing just beyond the kiosks. Quarter-sticks we called them when I was younger: dynamite. Year after year, it is the firework of choice for people intent on losing fingers and sight. The mighty concrete Rossiya trembled every few minutes as someone

set off the (as Lucia calls them) dinomito. She
likes to empower her comments with Italian swear
words to show the extent things bother her.
Vaffanculo! ... dinomito!

I opened the window to the smell of vodka and gunpowder. There was no one for a hundred yards. Vodka stank on the breeze.

Theoretically, I figured, if the sky wasn't filled up with radioactive isotopes, it could rain alcohol tonight. The kiosks across the way buzzed with last minute consumers; every one of the shoppers was drinking. From my experience, it takes about an hour to do the whole kiosk tour that way and it is quite expensive. I missed drinking, I missed gulping 12% beer and I missed balancing things on my forehead. I missed feeling that cozy feeling, missed that spring in my step and I missed being the funniest, happiest, and most charming person around. How can something so good be so bad? No, I was entering the New Year sober; excited but contained.

The New Years trees everyone has been buying off trucks are mostly sold. Here's the concept: If you can't afford a whole tree...you buy a branch. They cut apart the trees to sell branches. Of course good trees are hard to come by.

In four and a half hours Russia, West will pass into that celebration known as the New Year and things current will be a millennium in the past. Nationally, the year was marred with tragedy. From sinking submarines to building collapses, lost satellites to target bombings, mass deaths from the cold to Chechnyan checkmates.

The New Year in Russia is their precious holiday. Communism crippled Christmas, and Easter was allowed only as the sign of Spring. The state always promoted the New Year as their gift to the people. It is a true celebration with no guilt. Potential, change, something better, ships to come in, sons to come home….

Lucia just arrived... 20:00 hours. She's always a good couple of hours early. My French is now better than when I left immersion school twelve years ago. It is more natural and fluid than I ever considered possible because my grades in school didn't reflect my current talents. But I said 'I love you' in three languages to three different women and meant it three different ways.

I reminded Lucia we said we'd quit smoking at midnight. She had forgotten. If you've ever seen an Italian flatline in profanity for ten minutes, you'll know what I had to witness. It is impressive though not all that becoming. She smokes more than me; a feat in itself. She did not want to chew my Copenhagen tobacco and she did not want any nicotine gum. She said she'd stick to the agreement. *Porca vacca... nicotine gumma?*

New York hasn't woken up the ball yet and here we are at New Years in less than two hours. Russian clocks by nature don't run well. One of the most abundant of all Russian stores is the *Remont-Chasov* or clock repair. So the New Years moment is kind of spread over a half hour.

The doorbell cackled. Marina and her new boyfriend just arrived. Igor has a real bad cold. Thanks for coming Igor. They are spreading a tablecloth and cleaning test-tube shaped glasses. The TV is on. The room is arguing over which channel the countdown is on. One or Two. We are watching Two and flipping back to One every so often. Oleg and Alina arrived. Oleg loves me, he smokes my pipe, wears my fedora, gives me his federal LDPR business card holder, and looks through my clothes. It is hugs, two-cheeked kisses, good lucks all around.

The flat is nearly full. Elena, her man Valeri, Alina and Oleg, Marina, Sasha, and Igor are loud and drinking alcohol that will render them the funniest, happiest and most charming people around. Valeri is balancing things on his forehead. I am having tea. There are broccolis of different colours and something that looks like it was accidentally caught in a net. A classic Russian New Years film *Gentelmyene Oodachee* is on Channel Two. Garland is now draped the length of the fridge and little dangling shiny things are hanging from every bare hook. The Czech-made lights are strobing and the women won't let me in the kitchen.

The clock in Spasikaya tower at the Kremlin tolled off twelve bells on channel One as we merrily exchanged glances. It was a true look of friendship as we stared round the room at midnight. On the final great clang, I coiled arms with Lucia, toasted her *santé* and gave her a kiss that split her shoes. We watched President Putin address the country from Red Square. As Putin faded away, the NEW Russian Anthem was sung. That was a big deal. Someone had added new, official words to it. But all the vodka-flooded voices in my flat broke into the old lyrics and goose-stepped down the hallway. I pointed out to everyone it was this day in history in 1998 that Russia knocked three zeroes off the national currency under a long-planned currency reform. I can be such a party animal sober.

The fireworks had risen to a crescendo by midnight. Serge, a friend of Marina's, dropped by at twelve-thirty. He heard the firecrackers outside and said it sounded like Chechnya. Then he laughed in vodka coughs. I laughed only because he did. With the rapid coils burning through strings of finger-thick crackers, it *did* sound like Chechnya. He's going there in seven months. But only for two years he says. If only one could buy that optimism.

The doorbell yelped at one. Marina had invited her ex-boyfriend SashaZ to my place. She was not available when he rang. I hadn't met him and didn't know he was coming over. He explained that he had dated Marina for a time and then discovered he was gay. 'I suspected she had that ability,' I said to make conversation but it turned into an uncomfortable pause. SashaZ was quite an interesting person. His English was the best I'd heard in the city. SashaZ had been to most of Europe and he'd done it hitch-hiking. He'd travelled farther than the rest of the Russians in the room combined. He vacationed in Dubai twice a year, he surfed the internet more than me and he smoked pot. He pulled me down the cold apartment staircase and into the dark backyard near the dumpsters.

'You must... Russia's finest,' he said sparking his lighter at a joint. 'You aren't drinking, I can tell. You aren't drunk. By now you'd be balancing things on your forehead.'

'The last time I smoked pot in a foreign country, I got locked into a closet with my skeletons. It took two exorcisms and a pizza to get me out.'

'It is a New Year, a new Millennium Brant... take it.'

To the Russian authorities, drugs are like donating weapons to the Chechnyans. If you get caught, you'll likely have prison nurses cutting up your food for the rest of your life. You are the enemy. Not because you are enjoying a small piece of escapism in an un-escapism-friendly country but because you are challenging Authority. One could get 25 years in prison for telling an improper joke under Stalin, ten years for stealing a potato to feed your family, so few people were willing to risk life, limb and their freedom by smoking pot. Ganja was just as evil and punishable as cocaine or heroin. Not much going on at 4:20 am here. I looked at SashaZ and took the joint from him. I took in a sharp drag and held it, determined to make the sober night a thing of the past. SashaZ was smiling with approval. I exhaled.

'Holy shit that is bad!' I said.

'Bad as in good?' SashaZ asked. 'Colloquial?'

'Awful.'

'Awful as in good?' SashaZ asked. 'Slang? Vernacular? Idiomatic?'

'As in unsmoke-able, that taste... it's laced with fecal matter... bovine, dairy bovine. Late harvest.'

'You don't like it?' he asked surprised.

'SashaZ I come from British Columbia... Pot is our biggest industry. $7 billion a year, and wheat, our leading legal crop, is only $3 billion. We grow the best in the world... this... this is shit. I wish you could experience what my neighbour grew before the power company found him because... why are my hands glowing?'

'Aha,' said SashaZ 'I admit it may taste inferior to what you are used to but let's see if you can count to one without getting distracted.'

I was stoned at Mach 4. I felt my hair rush back and my toenails curl. My face felt like it'd been hit by a screen door. SashaZ came and leaned on me with a 'heh-heh'. We both dropped. There was mesmerizing dialogue in that cold night. It was as if we were brothers, separated at birth with a lifetime to catch up on. The pot accelerated an immediate friendship and within minutes we had a plan to sail to Monaco in a stolen sail-boat called *Monaco Or Bust*. As we sat on a long log in the freezing cold, people started leaving my party, some with pieces of my furniture. Oleg came out wearing my trench coat and fedora. I insisted we go in and rejoin the crowd. SashaZ lit up another joint and coaxed me into it once again. I couldn't believe it. I was smoking pot in Russia. I quickly remembered to be paranoid and couldn't shake it, all as per usual. But suddenly everyone belonged to the KGB which put an intense angle on the rest of the night.

There was food. Russians make 4.7 times the amount that actually gets eaten. Everyone in my flat sang, danced on the landing outside, swapped kisses on cheeks and watched the colourful fireworks browing the Rossiya. Alina felt unwell. Oleg drove his wife home and then showed up at 4am with Tsvetlana. He was drunk and had to introduce us because she spoke eight or nine words of English. Tsvetlana, a little shy to be the object of Oleg's praises, slowly recited the days of the week. Oleg, proud of showing off his mistress, drove away in the manner drunk men do when they're trying to impress another woman. SashaZ sat in the corner. Marina asked him if he was still gay. He told her he was.

At 04:40 only Lucia and I were left. She had been bubbling with champagne all night. Then she succumbed to heavy eyelids. Waking up people is one of the few pleasures I get from not drinking. So I woke her up. She had a look in her eyes like I had cured her ill mother. The room was a mess. There were empty vodka and tonic bottles strewn about the plates of fish, kolbasa, and a jellied mess that actually absorbed light. It all had to be protected from escapee roaches so I spent an hour taping the cheap tin foil back together and cleaned up stuff I'd only have to clean up later. Lucia watched me work then planted her forehead into the living room sofa. I stared at the dark road outside, the trams and the sparse traffic, for a half hour waiting for the sunrise to light; my Czech-made lights were spent. A little reflection on the past and a little ditty about the future. Fireworks rumbled on.

At seven, Alina phoned asking where Oleg was. I stretched the phone cord and peered out the peephole. Nope, he's not out there. Well this is not a good thing, I thought. Lucia was woken up for interpretation. She screamed and Alina screamed too and if I understood anything she said, it was 'Tsvetlana speaks English'. Lucia covered the phone and said in French that a divorce was imminent. This was gossip in its most immediate form.

I looked out my living room windows at the sunrise and

wondered 'Why am I the only one in Voronezh with three semi-stable relationships?'

The Russian Christmas seven days later was touted as another reason to stumble around and lose your keys. No one took it well when I called it OrthoChristmas. In the mucky Lenin Square, there were carnival rides and trailers. Everyone had been watching the ornament-adorned tree being raised, and the rides going up before Lenin's face for the past few weeks. It was like a typical American country fair except it was in Russia and it was -22C. Anya and I took a horse and cart around Lenin Square. The big tree, the dream of all Voronezhians, the spirit of their season, was undergoing spasms of light. The square was lined with unsound children's rides, haunted houses, 'Guess-your-weight-for-a-ruble' babushkas, cotton candy stands, and shooting galleries.

The night before was Anya's Christmas Eve. We stood for an hour and a half in the muggy station waiting for a train that never came. Her family was waiting in that seven-kilometres-from-any-transport village. She had that distance to bear on Christmas Eve. As a last resort, she spent the Russian Christmas Eve in my flat. The banks of apartment windows were aglow with candles, the traditional 'vacancy' sign to the Virgin Mary.

Christmas in Russia is hosted by Father Frost or *Dyed Moroz* and his granddaughter *Snegourotchka*. They brave their way across Siberia, drawn by three horses, a *troika* if you will, to dispense gifts to all the young girls and boys. I explained to my classes that the wonderful Western version had elves, flying reindeer and a fat guy who slides down skinny chimneys. 'Reindeer can't fly…' they would respond (these are people who *know* reindeer). I answered I knew reindeer couldn't fly but little children didn't know. It was a fairy tale, like communism. 'So you tell young children that a man flies around with magical reindeer?' they would say. 'At least our stories have a semblance of truth. Father Frost *did* visit us'. This was true. Father Frost did visit children. (In fact, many companies still follow the Stalinist tradition of releasing someone to play Father Frost for the night.) He, accompanied by Snegourotchka, came around and knocked on doors. Gifts are given out to the parents as the children run to their rooms to sleep, having witnessed the deity of gift-giving for themselves. It was customary, in days gone by, to give Father Frost a shot of vodka but that was stopped by law a few years ago. Students recalled a drunk Father Frost as their first holiday memory. In the morning the children would race to see what Father Frost had left for them and on occasions they'd found him passed out or in a compromising position with Snegourotchka.

Someone fixed the streetlight outside on Koltsovskaya Street on December 31st and, for reasons unknown, the one on the landing outside my flat on December 25th. It was truly a grand time in my piece of Voronezh. You see, if you need a bulb in your apartment, you take the one from the landing. Most of the apartments are privately owned and no landlord would ever consider the external landing any of their concern. And so most stairways are dark. This fixture must have been a gift from one of two doors adjacent to me; the drunk who owes me two hundred rubles or the woman I can hear crying through the wall at night.

On another positive note, with the new bulb I could now find my keys and the three locks in a fifth the time, enough time to give anyone the slip. I felt many times that someone was following me and the enlightening news from my students that the FSB routinely went through my apartment gave me an insecurity I'd never known. Sometimes I closed a strand of hair in the door intent on confirming whether this was a reality or just a tale to keep a foreigner in order. Most times the hair was there when I returned home. Sometimes it was not. I was suspicious at the motives of the FSB. I became distrustful of the militsia on the streets. If my apartment was bugged then the officials knew who I was seeing, which lady would make a better wife, and just how horrible my singing voice was. If I farted in my flat, I pictured a bunch of agents with headphones laughing in a van parked down the street. When you come to a country such as Russia, you surrender such rights on the tarmac. I gave up caring and often left for the day with my Norwegian death metal CDs playing on repeat.

The Christmas season disappeared quicker than Santa entering this airspace. The churches that had been sweeping the air with smoking icons have retreated indoors to tend to their candles. Tinsel was stuck in the muddy lake that had overtaken Voronezh. It was soon January 14th, the Orthodox New Years. All those resolutions that had been lost to the underdogs of courage in the last two weeks got a fresh new start. This calendar thing, where Russia follows the Julian calendar and the Russian Orthodox dates coupled with the Old Soviet holidays...it makes every day a reason to celebrate because if you don't, you just might miss one. Incidentally, the Hebrew date was 19 Tevet 5761. I fear one day there may be only one language in the world, but one calendar would actually be a good thing.

The Orthodox holiday didn't have much in the way of festivities. There was no work and no one phoned to wish me into the New Year. I spent the day writing and watching drunk people meander down the street. I had found a small shop which sold incense, books, and calming CDs. It sat behind the Rossiya, completely encircled by a puddle. I had to evacuate my flat after I burned orange peel incense too soon after a stick of sandalwood. While I waited for the room to clear, I went over to the kiosks and bought another nail clipper, cigarettes and a fat cigar. Lucia and I had started smoking again with valid reasons that we agreed to keep to ourselves. I clipped my nails and lit the stogie, filling the air with ribbons of Cuban smoke. The streets were fairly mushy and the sidewalks were jagged and cracked. This was the New Year and the country was filled with hope and promise. I smoked the cigar for a good five blocks until I was coughing far more than I was enjoying myself. I walked by the clock repair store, the watch repair store, the banks, and the film place. I raced a tram and crossed over to the bread lady. I liked her. She had never steered me wrong. Never had I had a stale loaf of French bread; frozen yes, but never stale. I tossed away the cigar and munched down on doughy mouthfuls of bread. From the road I could see my flat and the smoke being tugged out my open window. Incense is a very tricky thing; making combinations was like mixing medications.

When I was eleven and first learning French, it was obvious to me and my classmates that we'd get nowhere in the language until we first mastered the art of swearing. This was true, too, with Russian. There are times you may want to infer that some-one's parents were brother and sister and there are times you want to interrupt people with a loud exclamation that will make you the immediate focus. Russian *matb*, as the swearing dialect of taboo invectives is known, is actually its own language and one can even tell where another person is from by the dialect they curse in. Once, casually in public, I used one of the swear words I knew. I stopped traffic. It seems the word I used was far more inappropriate than any English equivalent. I learned quickly to use such words only in close quarters and even then to watch my mouth and context. I will however impart a word that I feel I can't hurt anyone by passing on: *amanskizkizballa.* This is a Kazak word that'll make everyone on an Almaty street think you are a sailor who just stubbed his toe.

Marina was still dating Igor. Igor is skinny and tall and covered with a mess of short black hair. Igor was always broke, always hungry and always a few bottles of cheap beer short of sober. They frequented my flat because they both live with their parents and I am a good friend who will let them screw on my couch while I go for a walk. Igor came over for that purpose and to check his emails. Igor doesn't have many people to email so one night while he was studiously investigating his inbox's abundance of cheap Viagra offers, Marina and I talked about her working overseas. At thirty-five and single, save for Igor, she didn't think she'll ever leave Russia again. Quoting an appropriate Russian anecdote she said, 'We were put on this earth for our previous sins; the country you live in reflects their severity.' I felt sorry for Marina as her hopes were dashed by age and citizenship.

Igor soon became a piece of furniture. Three or four nights a week, he would ring the horrific doorbell and enter alone, with Marina, or a new woman. He was quite a lady's man and Marina faded as an A-list girlfriend a month on. Igor worked part-time as a DJ at a club and the women he began bringing over were quite stunning. Though if he wasn't with Marina, he would convey to me with a finger to his thick Russian lips that I was to be quiet about the subject matter who, incidentally, lingered with perfume that would stick to my flat for days.

With Igor I made one of my most worthwhile friendships; he was a low maintenance house guest. There was a chasm of language we filled with sign language, affirmative nods and hearty laughs. We managed to get quite intellectual with the help of the dictionary. Igor knew no English except the alphabet and this he used to buy CDs. My Russian was pure and straight, but limited. Of our two languages, Russian prevailed. His father was a pilot who flew from Moscow to Dubai. Igor saw little of him. He said it'd always been that way. Igor and his mother lived an hour from downtown by tram, and their apartment, I gathered, was tight for two. Igor's taste in music, as he was young and a disc jockey, was annoyingly electronic and quite different from mine. Often we sat in silence.

Because of my mother tongue situation, everyone wanted time with me. I understood the students trying to drag me to clubs or out for days in the countryside, for these would be excursions in English. An English classroom with a Russian teacher is like a mock battle. With me, they had to use English and could not just pretend they knew it. But of all the people I felt most comfortable with, Igor was the one guy who didn't have nor desperately want English. He knew that English was an essential tool but he never asked for anything other than help deciphering his spam. We just sat around smoking my cigarettes, drinking my tea, using my computer, and listening or not listening to music. I knew an objective of his was the internet but still I appreciated his company all the same. He liked mine. I know it gave him a chance to parade his new girlfriends around and I know it was frequently me who gave him bus money home from the city but of all the friends that pressed me for time, Igor got the most.

One night I went to the theatre to see Milorad Pavich's *Forever and a Day*. Lucia explained the story in French. Between her asides, I managed to follow some of the Russian dialogue myself. Not enough to laugh along, but each familiar word was

like an old friend. The theatre was small and built into a corner
of what had been a gigantic theatre during the Soviet times. The
building, set on a few acres of bad vegetation, housed different
rooms for different theatre activities. The great foyer had thick
pillars holding up a high ceiling.

The play was perfect in every way. Five actors shared parts
over the small stage and spent two hours in a light show I
decided was better than Motley Crue in '88 and '93 put together.
Watching from my seat in a bowed third row, the talent was
beyond anything I'd ever seen. For an equivalent $1.50 to get
in, the cast gave far more than they were earning. They weren't
actors for money. Genuine, unselfish talent is hard to come by. I
was not one to properly judge the intricacies of fine theatre, I
could only point to what appealed to me. There wasn't a
moment where I could point out a lapse of script or missed
synchronicity in their step. Perhaps if I spoke Russian fluently I
would have found something close to an error. But I think not.

My grandfather had sent me Canadian Remembrance Day items
and clippings by post and they arrived three months late. He
sent a poppy and a list of WWII relatives in the who, what,
when and where format. Voronezh has a long history of battling
the Germans and the scars are deep, open, and sensitive.
Fascism is a word that is spoken with scowls and flared nostrils.
Russians have always known loss, tragedy, and misfortune. In
World War II Russia lost thirty to forty million people to battle,
disease, and starvation. I had been to the local museum with its
dented Nazi helmets, destroyed Messersmit fuselages and anti-
aircraft guns. I had climbed on 'Joseph Stalin' tanks, knocked on
chipped turrets, and gripped the worn steering wheel of a 1940s
rocket launcher. To see the display is to see the symbols of
capture, defeat, and reclamation by a united country. All a

representation of what Russia was. The Remembrance Day reminders from my grandfather now took on an entirely different meaning, something years of my grade schooling didn't offer. Reality.

As I welcomed my fourth month in Russia, it was exam time and I was free to do as I pleased, relatively speaking. I could not take a taxi to Kazakhstan, no one would let me drive their cars in the snow, and my trip across the Black Sea to Turkey in a Kon-tiki based vessel seemed dim. My brother Sean and his fiancé Hilary had saved their money for a year in Europe. They were poised to leave Canada within a week. There was no plan for them to visit Russia because of the paperwork involved. I could, on my visa, leave and enter Russia once. In an email, Sean had alluded to Istanbul as a potential point of meeting.

I needed to find something to do. The students spent their days studying and taking their semester tests. I boiled a kettle of h2oFe7 and brewed a room-perfuming chai from India - actually an area in dispute with Pakistan. Dangerous tea. That week put an end to the exams and half of my time commitment in Voronezh. The early results of the English marks were positive, which was a mark of personal pride. Students had opened their hearts and lives to me. Much of that came in fragments of structure and theory I'd given them. The broad Russian approach was to have a Russian teacher hammer out instruction in a stunted English accent while reading from photocopied British books. And even she or he may have never met a native speaker of the language. The polarities were visible. To have had a foreigner teach you English was a milestone in a linguist student's life here.

Teaching in Russia had other riches like hearing a new student's first full sentence, overcoming pronunciation obstacles and smiles in return for correction. I also learnt the power of humility. I was told in a healthy challenge of ideals that one doesn't *walk into a monastery with one's own rules* (don't ever ask a class of Russians how they'd choose to 'die'... even if you have twenty unscripted minutes before you and it looks like it's a sure out). Ah well.

Other teachers often sat in on my classes to spur debate over dictionary meanings, launch dumb things like 'second-person phrasal predicates' at me, or just to rest. The way the classes have previously been taught was simply Soviet-strategy; these students were mechanics of the language. They knew things about *my* language I never knew existed. One night with the sixth years, we somehow went from 'global warming' to 'verb inflections' in the space of a few confusing minutes.

'English inflects verbs by affixation to mark the third person singular in the present tense, that is with an 's', and the present participle with 'ing,'' said Nadya.

'Yes,' I said agreeably. '… it does do that.'

'English short adjectives are inflected to mark comparative and superlative forms,' Zoe said.

'With 'er' and 'est' respectively…' added Marya almost innocently.

'English is… pretty neat that way,' I said.

Every word, concept or idea that my students have about English was their own. They've earned it. They deserve the language.

Anya's babushka died. A sobbing, stuttering voice on the phone said that her grandmother had been enjoying the night until death set in. She died in her chair. In the village. In remote Russia. Grafskaya isn't a pleasant place to live let alone to die.

'*Ladno*… I must go… how to say… wash the body.'

'Well then…uh', I replied with no idea how to follow it, 'I'll see you in class tomorrow... keep that chin up… turn that frown upside-… um, bye.'

Anya and I went to the Church of the Shroud and lit candles for the ceremonial ninth-day dead. There weren't many people there as we stood our candles among a hundred others of various heights. It was a poetic act. Anya looked so mature in her headscarf and fur coat. A monk started chanting in 64th beats to Old Orthodox Scripture. Two old women in the corner were sparring in prayer fights. I was scanning the icons and chipped walls waiting for lightning. I gave Anya a very kind kiss. Every one of my senses was full. Babushka got whatever the candle was meant for.

I took a look around at the other people hovering near their candles lit for their dead. It was a melancholy group. Russian churches are built for the living and the dead alike. They look poised for a wedding ceremony combined with an ultra-grieving memorial service. They are stern and omniscient, sturdy and trustworthy. Anya tearfully watched the candle burn its length. Finally it was snuffed out by the pool of wax that encircled it.

On a miserably cold and grey morning, Lucia and I went to watch the final exams of the state's folklore singers. It was in an Arts Council building that had seen better days. While waiting in the foyer, we stood whispering in French. Lucia didn't mind looking foreign. She was comfortable exerting a strong Italian presence wherever she went. It probably had something to do with World War II. I, on the other hand, wanted to fade to obscurity and pretend I was another cog in a Russian process.

We looked for a place to smoke and ended up outside until the cold numbed our fingers and returned us indoors. There was

a piano that had been pulverized by use. Though the exposed
keys and strings were left intact, it could hardly play a note.
Lucia told me not to take a picture of it. She said there were too
many people around who might chastise us for making light of
it. But it was too tempting.

I'd never seen a musical instrument in its final stage of
decay. It is possible this piano was still used for weekly choir
practice. My flashbulb ate up the dark room, producing
shadowy Russian bodies. There were murmurs but no one
approached us. There is an unspoken rule in Eastern European
countries: one does not expose the obvious signs of poverty.
You never say, 'Shit Vladimir, half that building has collapsed
and there are still families/businesses/political opposition
offices in it'. Nope, as a visitor, you do not say such things…
those are for Vladimir to point out.

A troop of Russian singers in full traditional dress filed past
us and mounted the stairs. They slipped behind a curtain and
only once they were well hidden were we told to go down the
stairs to the small auditorium. Noticing that we were foreigners,
a small man with a limp gave us preferred seating behind a man
with a tall hat.

We were exposed to a battle of songs between the final two
teams. The brilliance in the old Russian traditions, the songs
that swept over the fields as the women reaped wheat, or that
were sung after meals in the villages, was a wonderful exhibit
of hundreds of years of rural custom. With twelve singers each,
the highly decorated women choirs sang such favorites as *We
Go To Mother Volga*, *Harvested Hay,* and *Oh You Soldiers'
Wives*. The costumes they wore had survived centuries without
change. The women wore colourful red skirts with decorative
needlework, white puffy blouses, and red headscarves. The
most symbolic piece hung from their necks. Among the beads
and chains were rings of patterned fabric that told the histories,

with precision, of where the woman's family was from. Each woman wore her past. The men, of which there were only two per team, had long white tunics and bright red sashes. They were there to play the accordion or pan-flute.

A month after the Gregorian Christmas, I had received two-fifths of my presents from home. My parents had sent my parcels via post and I felt certain they'd be in the Federation and unwrapped by late December. This was not the case. Surely by this time they could be opened, eaten or played with. The Russian Postal System isn't a particularly efficient means of handling mail. They seem to do well delivering small envelopes but anything from a small packet and upwards is likely to cause them problems. It will invariably be sent to a postal outlet which will have strange hours of operation. And inside there, at 2am, at the end of a long and grumpy queue, you will be told since you didn't pick up your parcel in the allotted four hour limit, the package has been sent to another postal station with even wonkier hours. But, you say, if something was sent AIR from Canada and it is over two months late, inevitably it is sitting somewhere. If you raise this point to the person behind the counter, they will not reply. To them your theory is absurd and your presence is now unwanted. Where is it sitting? Where is it being mixed up with the GROUND parcels? These questions remain unanswered. This is Russia, this is the system. And to date I've not come across any distraught postal employees or customers going on shooting rampages. Maybe the crazy people are in control of the AIR packages.

Anya came over and attempted suicide. She arrived in tears, shaking, swooning, and claiming to have taken a bunch of pills of something I couldn't define from the Cyrillic label. I read it as acidi-acyetlsalicylicik. 0,5 grams each. I found her outside my building as I was leaving to the market. I held her by the shoulders and guided her upstairs. She sat there crying, sniffling into my favourite pillow. With nowhere else to go and no one else to confide in, she came to me. She told me her aunt had just chased her around her house with a butchers' knife. Russia has a high suicide rate and I listened to Anya's reasons for this lonely choice. I soon found that her habitual depression was more than just a symptom; she had stuff to back it up. Her mother had twice tried to kill her as a baby. She had been an unwanted pregnancy and she was told that all through her childhood.

Her mother became a prostitute and her father a common drunk. She had been cared for by her militsia-employed uncle but he was killed in the line of duty a year ago. She had moved in with her grandparents and the aunt. Her aunt had always been jealous of the relationship she had shared with her uncle, and to this postmortem day she resented it. She resented it so intensely that physical fights between them broke out all the time. On rare occasions the knives came into play.

I offered her my day, my night, my Monday, after three o'clock Tuesday, Wednesday until Natasha arrived. How could a small world like Voronezh disturb someone to this extent? This young woman was destroyed at 22 years old and she'd never been anywhere. She'd never been 'away from it all', this life was there waiting for her every morning. She was despondent, often incoherent yet resolute. With nowhere else to go she came to my flat to kill herself.

She emptied the rest of the tablets into a glass of water. When she left to vomit, I removed as much medication as I could with the spoon. It still looked potent. I couldn't let her drink it as it was but, if she was serious, dumping it out would have made her seek out some other means, somewhere else. I wanted to be sure she wasn't using me for something. I mean she was now homeless. And she did come to my flat. Was she not expecting me to talk her out of suicide? She was scattered, her mind wasn't working well. She spoke verbose Russian to the walls in a fluent manner that led me to believe I wasn't supposed to understand her. She rambled on and on and then phoned Nona. When she hung up, she said Nona wanted her to meet at the kiosks. She promised to return and die shortly thereafter.

I didn't know if I should exceed the teacher/student line that presumably the Russian Education system ethics had drawn between us. Surely I risked being fired. I couldn't phone anyone or I'd blow my cover. I decided to try and have her stay with me awhile. A thousand rubles said the only way to save her was to give her a promise. This relationship was now unavoidably deep and I couldn't pretend it was just a 'thing' we did. I seemingly faced a guarantee of 'forever' or losing a good girl to suicide, today, tomorrow, or the next day. Russians are a dramatic and determined people, if only to make a point. I knew she'd drink the glass.

She didn't drink the glass. When she returned from meeting Nona, she sat down on the couch with her shaking hands between her knees and her head twitching. I learned that she suffered from a rare nervous disorder, which frequently resulted in her shaking, trembling, and quivering. I had thought those actions were just an addition to her personality, like her dimples. But it was a bad disease that took her body and was ruining it and would in time kill her. We spoke about death and how final it all seemed. I made her laugh a time or two at my expense and tried unsuccessfully to make a joke at her expense. The first dose of pills had terribly upset her stomach. She threw up a few more times. The little foggy glass sat on the coffee table, fizzing with potential. I told her if she wasn't going to drink it, I was going to dump it down the sink. She left to vomit. Seizing the opportunity, I drained the cup in the kitchen.

Anya moved in to my flat with what I can only describe as a 'ton of shit'. Nona helped her carry over an assortment of multi-coloured cardboard boxes and straw bags. Anya knew she was only there for a 'while' to sort things out but she felt the need to bring all of her picture albums, personal hygiene effects and electrical appliances. She had summer clothes and winter clothes. She had not just 'moved in' but obviously 'moved out' as well. I piled her stuff in the eerie room in the back, split my wardrobe into sides, and threw her pillow beside mine. I was now living with an orphan, a farm girl in the big city, a student.

It had been my best week in Voronezh so far. It was -28C and the moment you inhaled, your tongue was sheet metal and your nose whistled. What made the week exceptional were my successes on the previous Monday. I had lectured the state's forty-two head English teachers for two hours at a major university in the suburbs. When I entered, Tatyana beamed with happiness. She thought this would be an exciting event. I was a bundle of nerves. I was taken to the teacher's lounge and fed a horrible cup of instant coffee. I forgot about the whole coffee/caffeine/bowel thing because my mind was awash with a thousand thoughts. Tatyana was trying to make me feel like Billy Graham but I saw right through her. She was trying to build my confidence. Then I reached the grounds at the bottom of my mug. I had a solar flare of strength.

'I hope that was a fart'.

'*Izvenitse*?' Tatyana said.

'… uh, I'm eager to start…'

I was ushered down a dark hall, along a dark corridor and

into a bright classroom. The teachers put down their pens, ended their whispers and faced forward. They spanned every weight and age and looked nauseatingly educated. I began.

Many had never met a native English speaker. And they themselves had only seen each other once every five years. They collected in Voronezh to trade insights, acquire more training, and listen to lectures. As well, they took part in an exam that tells of traditional Soviet practice. Their result on the test would be reflected in their wage, and their status, until the next exam five years later.

I was there because Tatyana thought my presence would make an excellent opportunity for the teachers. She had arranged everything and was now sitting in the first row with her beguiling smile. On the board I jokingly wrote 'Englich is you're keys to the werld' and stood innocently beside it. It was meant to be an ice-breaker but it didn't go over well. In fact, I discovered that many of them had horrible English problems themselves.

I spoke and answered their questions and Tatyana began prompting me with her own questions when I ran short of ideas. Much of what I said clarified or distinguished North American English from the British that most were used to. I would catch them taking notes or writing in their books. I had started out shaky but finished two hours prepared to go for a third. They couldn't believe I bounced off the walls, juggled ceramics, showed a picture of my dog, and got them to do the 'wave'.

Tatyana initiated a small round of clapping at the end and I was led away for a tea. After conversing with the teachers, Tatyana came into the boardroom and told me they were exceptionally pleased with my homily though many commented on my gesticulating, which I realized only then just how much I had done. It was Russian style not to use your hands in front of a class because it presupposed you didn't have the words to fill the meaning. I was a manic mime. I used my hands to describe, illustrate, and articulate a point. Tatyana, in her fifties, with three jobs and six kids, was once reported for her gesticulating in a formal complaint launched by several students. The head people, faceless and nameless I know them to be, sat in on her classes and then disciplined her. Enter me.

I had a student at the university who had me perplexed from the first class. He, being the only male, stood out from the others. But it was more of the person he was. Pavel was over six feet tall and always wore a trench coat. His curly brown hair waved over his long nose. I could tell by his stern eyes that he was paying attention during class yet he rarely participated. For a few classes he just sat there, watching from the back of the class. I tried to involve him in the discussions but it was easy to tell he preferred not to be called upon. One night after we'd wrapped up and I was headed home, Pavel asked if I minded if he walked part way with me. As the university fell behind us, Pavel started crying. He grappled at his knapsack and shoved a hand inside. Wiping tears, he handed over a pile of papers, all of which were in Russian. These were, he confided, all of his writings. I asked him why he was giving me them and he started crying the way a man cries: sniffling and with the constant wiping of the eyes to keep pride. Pavel confronted me with a request. He took his time and warned me that an important question was coming. Could I get him into the United States? Or Canada? Pavel told me that he had spent two years in Chechnya, that he'd seen every friend killed, and that he needed to know that I could get him overseas or he would simply enlist and die in a suicide promise in Chechnya. As he wept, I knew he would. He could not fit back in to Russia.

I patted Pavel on the back and promised everything would get better. I was lying. All the odds were against him. I couldn't guarantee him even a shot at Canada. All I knew was that he could take the regular, legal way into Canada, like every other immigrant that doesn't come on a rusty freighter. I didn't tell Pavel that straight away. I said I would look online at possibilities. His short-story writings were all he had that had any worth and he had just given them to me in case he ended up going back to Chechnya.

Pavel walked me almost to my apartment. His eyes cleared up. I promised to see what there was on the internet - perhaps I'd find the annual American Green Card Lottery and Pavel could go for that. Or maybe there was an exchange program and Pavel could go for that. I looked at Pavel, part boy-part man, and I knew he didn't look like the type of person to cry easily.

Whenever I saw the time on my laptop's taskbar at 19:17, I thought of that year when Lenin took his first step toward the future of the country I now lived in. The cold Russian winter was a gulag of its own. The icicles were dropping as the temperature surfaced and hovered around zero. Real honest-to-god icicles, like in cold movies. The last days had been the Brass Monkey ones. It was cold enough to sleep clothed. And my thermometer froze.

One front room window wouldn't close all the way and it was necessary to leave the kitchen window open for gas fumes lest a leak expire the unsuspecting sleepy guy about to light the kettle for his morning's first mug of chai.

I had now lived in my flat in Russia for longer than most places I'd lived anywhere. Some things still amuse me and me alone. The oven was so small that pans and food only fit in on an angle. The jets from the gas must be lit by sticking a hand beyond the reach of your average person. A babushka could simply combust if not wary. Turning on the gas and pointing a lit match down to the seeping jets was the only way to start that incredibly stupid appliance. Every single time I'd tried this, it became a reason for going hungry. My cheap scarves had a flashpoint of 50 degrees Celsius. Withdrawing a scorching meal with the Russian oven mitts was another challenge. I melted the plastic tablecloth to the table once. I almost did it twice but I remembered the first time and burnt the paint on the windowsill instead.

I continued with the treatments for my neck pain. After sixty injections, all taken in the rump, I was seemingly cured. There were many days, many treatments, and far travels to see the good doctor in every catalogued kind of weather. Marina escorted me each time though I knew my way there soon after we started. She seemed to enjoy seeing me with my shorts around my ankles and Dr. Yakov lining up the needles with my *zadnitsa*. The massages I endured were painful. Yakov's hands were strong and he kneaded my muscles into pulp. But in the final treatment (where my head was supported by a weight thrown over a door) I was told that all my ills had been modified or corrected. My spine was now straight and my muscles were sufficiently strong to keep it that way for a time. Over the years I had tried a lot of solutions and nothing had ever worked for more than a day. Yakov came through for me and I would not experience my regimen of pain for a very pleasant six months. None of a dozen other doctors had produced that kind of remission. I had paid Yakov a measly sixty dollars and for that I was a new person, a person without pain.

The respect that Lucia and I shared was estranged from the norm. I fancied using my French all the time. She gave that language back to me. She made relevance of my six years of French immersion in grade school. God knows the French language skills had never helped me in Western Canada. Of all places, here I was in southern Russia flipping tenses and screwing around with predicates like it was nobody's business.

Lucia and I had, it seemed, been sharing nightmares. She explained that she'd dreamt she was back in Italy and that her Russia experience had ended horribly. I was having similar depressing nights and waking soaked through the sheets. I'd dreamt of losing all I'd made of my life in Voronezh. Lucia was a strong woman, fighting her own past and for a while I let her battle mine. Russia was Lucia's in a different way. Russia wanted an Italian teacher. Not many countries need Italian to manage their economic future but she was welcomed as a foreign oddity. She shared the parts of her heart that she could but there was still a few levels I never saw into. Lucia had given everything she had to teach in Russia. Working for waitress' tips, she arrived without travel insurance or a backup plan. There was no way she could afford to go home broken hearted. And the dreams made her nauseous.

Lucia's happier dream was to travel through Mongolia and teach in a small community. I searched the internet for jobs, specifically *Italian*, *teacher*, and *Mongolia*. Suddenly I saw the power of English. Lucia didn't have any English. She was thousands of words away from fluency. She was an Italian language teacher and had no chance of using her years of schooling in any place exotic. My opportunities were limited only by what I didn't know and couldn't bluff but Lucia was likely going home when her sojourn in Russia ended.

My flat was chilled enough to see my breath. The situation in Voronezh paled with other areas of Russia. A news report gave this update: 'In some regions, temperatures have fallen well below -50 Celsius, causing steel rails on the Trans-Siberian railway to fracture in the cold. Public television reported last week a total of 600,000 people were affected by poor heating in the Far East, and 18,000 people had no heating at all.' There was footage of families in Tomsk, Siberia all hovering around an iron for warmth. Gas, in private hands, had become very expensive but electricity, when it was working, was cheaper.

There was a small back room beyond my bedroom. There was no light and other than using the storage place for my luggage, I'd not ventured into it. One night when Anya was over at Nona's, I used my travel candle to probe the depths of the closet. At the very back I found two broken rotary-dial phones, three dead mice and a heater. I could not believe my luck. I put the phones on eBay and went back for the heater. It was steel and took two hands to carry out to the front room. It was orange. I gave it the name R2. There was one switch, On or Off. There was no control of the temperature and when R2 got going, there was a three foot radius of heat that would char. It had to sit in the middle of the room for safety. The temperature peaked and just when I'd started to think I would survive the winter, R2 died. Sparks leapt from the Siberian Death Mask/fuse box. I put fuses on my to-do list and parked R2 back in the small room.

Sergei came Sunday after Sunday and each time I could detect subtle differences in his progress toward speaking English. Like many Russians, his accent was stuck on several key sounds. We spent much time pronouncing 'three', 'what', and 'three-what'. Sergei was listening to the tapes at work, night after night. I admired his tenacity. If anyone was going to learn from the cassettes, it would be him. However hard he tried, and for all his persistence, he could still not overcome the lisps and lose the Russian gurgle that cost him certain words.

We spent hours running through the sequences and questions he'd likely asked in his phone-interview. The call was coming from a reputable firm based in Colorado that recruited workers from Russia. Sergei was intelligent and a certified computer programmer. There were side discussions in which he would try to convey to me the intricacies of computer programming. Much of the lexicon he used was English. We worked hard at all facets of the language so Sergei could convincingly pass his interview.

You can see the decay of youth. If a woman isn't married by twenty-four, pregnant by twenty-five and (barring war) a mother for the rest of her life, she is stained and talked about behind her back. She is 'beyond *the* age'. Such is Marina's situation. She is thirty-five, never married, and lives with her parents eight flights up in a cold, grey building. It's a hostile climb to grope along the broken railings, and stumble up well-worn stairs. She does it three times a day. They dry their laundry from the porches. (That is quite the sight. Russian underwear I mean. It's built for space walks.) Anyway, Marina was adept in English, she hates to be corrected, remembers fondly she taught Russian at Cambridge for a year, but was now into her ninth year teaching English back in Russia in a job she hated. She daily cringed as she marched off to class. It was because that was as far as she could go. The competition for proficient interpreters was fierce and her best, youngest years were gone. The walls that were built around her by not getting married and bearing a child are Russian dogma. Her monthly stipend of 600 rubles ($18 US) barely allowed her to buy a chocolate bar let alone consider two. Her 'future' as a concept was doomed to repeat the past. Ergo... babushka.

Russians usually don't smile in photographs. They don't naturally enjoy being photographed bearing expression, exposing emotions, or gleaming their golden-toothed bicuspids, but they do pose. One day I challenged the traditional Russian style, and took photos of everything from a butcher axing pieces off a cow-on-hook to caviar spilling from a splayed sturgeon. I snapped off shots of beggars and gypsies. I took shots of the tram conductors, the ladies who sold me my cheese, strays in a dumpster feeding frenzy, and threw my arm and camera inside a CD kiosk and got a picture from the inside. My photo albums would now be more exciting. Looking through the staff's photo albums was a boring trip through expressionless friends in vodka-stained days in Voronezh or vacations to Sochi on the Black Sea. The irony is that Russian photographers, career and private alike, are possibly the best in the world. The litany of photography magazines at the newspaper kiosks were filled with passionate artists, diverse perspectives, and their talents with a pirated copy of Photoshop.

Waiting is a Russian custom. You can stand 'in queue' for up to half an hour to buy film, get a new door handle, or pay the cashier. This is a Russian transaction: you peruse your choices, occasionally asking what part of the animal that piece is from or if it is fresh. You call the sales woman, *'dyevooshki!'* (literally 'girl, c'mere') which is not at all considered rude. She gives you the price for the item on a small piece of paper. You march to the end of the cashier's line and pay through a small bullet-proof window, receive your change on a plate with a *chet*, a receipt saying you've paid the proper amount. And finally you return to the line-up between you and your purchase.

You wait.

'Dyevooshki!'

She cuts, weighs, and wraps your purchase in between helping out the louder people. That is for one goddamn item. Good luck if you brought a list. And there are no shopping carts in Russia. That arm of science didn't get any funding. Everyone travels with similar plastic bags. Lipton, L'Oreal, Disney read their sides. The mafia favour Disney cartoon bags while the babushka population prefers anything to do with feminine hygiene.

Russia has produced many great writers. I believe that is particularly due to the country they are from. Many must have thought, 'There is no way future generations are going to fucking believe... I shall write it down.' Russia is a stern and foreboding place. It always has been. Until the early 19th century, Europe considered Russia medieval. The rulers have always been harsh on the lower classes and, ironically, that is where the best of the writers have come from. Fyodor Dostoevsky, who said '*Taking a new step, uttering a new word, is what people fear most*' took hard, bitter steps himself. He was a split-decision away from being shot by a firing squad then granted a reprieve and sent to a Siberian hard-labour camp for ten years. Profoundly, he was able to write psychologically disturbing, probing works about his country's mental climate, his own challenges with faith, and his prison time. Alexander Solzhenitsyn was another who spent time in gulags and yet another who survived to not only write about the abuses and the conditions in prison, but to expose them to the world, receive the Nobel Prize for literature, and become one of the most respected writers of all time. (I've read *A Day In The Life Of Ivan Denisovitch* once a year at home to remind me how lucky I am to be able have a job that I hate.) Ayn Rand was Russian-born but moved to America at 19 with contempt for her homeland. It was likely those 19 years that gave her the ammunition to change the face of philosophy-by-literature. Anton Chekhov produced many short stories and plays that revealed the beating heart of Russia's emotions. And to round out the great writers, there is Boris Pasternak, the man who introduced the world to *Doctor Zhivago*.

Alexander Pushkin remains the national poet. In his preserved sense of beguiling and egotistical prose, Pushkin narrates his Russia, her folklore and the contemporary culture. Pushkin's fourth cousin, Leo Tolstoy, a noble, wrote *War and Peace* to cure Russian insomniacs. There are a great number of works, all of which deserve to be heard and read and reread. I purchased the finest copies I could find on Plexhanovskaya Street. People were selling their personal copies of *House of the Dead*, *Fathers and Sons*, selected poetry of Pushkin, or short stories of Chekhov. They were, of course, all in Russian and I was quite a distance from handling the deep metaphors, introspective imagery, and century-old literary construct. But I am genetically a book collector. Russian literature calms me. The writers, passionate about their craft, knew that a writer's mind is never to himself; that the credit of his life is behind every sentence. And when he writes a period, his sins are in it.

As for music, the world knows well of Russian abilities. Her share of classical is vast and diverse. Rachmaninoff, Tchaikovsky, Shostakovich, Prokofiev, Stravinsky - all famed composers served the epochs with their gifts. I love classical music, particularly Russian, and enjoyed many nights alone with a cup or six of chai while the masters played out their pieces on my small stereo. My eyes would glance around at my Russian surroundings. The music was at home. So, too, was I.

I also enjoy hard rock, heavy metal - the kind of industrial music that threatens your dreams and makes you want to shave the cat. I can switch between the two types of music with ease. I learned to appreciate Russian bands, some heavy and others sublime. Aria, DDT, Kino, Akvarium, Tatu, Ivanushki and so on. My tastes favoured the classics though. I would, in times of wonder or bouts of depression, put on my coat and walk the dark streets, smoking my pipe while my personal Russian recording device provided me with appropriate music. You don't have to look far to find depression in Russian music, old or new. It is there, like a staple to the generations. A lot of it makes you consider putting a Kalashnikov up to your temple (I think it's the treble that does it to people). But various others are tame, stable, and melodic. The wild feeling I felt when, covered in pipe smoke, I would shuffle through people on their hurried paths home, was elating. With Rachmaninov's *Concerto No. 3* or Valeri Meladze's *Kak Ti Krasiva Sevodnija*, I would march in heavy steps about my little Russian city. Passing the kiosks with their loaves of breads or sidestepping granite buildings with a column of busy women selling seeds, all of it was magical and so 'Russian' that it made me run home and email people about what I'd just seen.

I was now a more common sight in the community. I still stared down many people when I went out. I wore my fedora most of the time. At first I was a little afraid, timid to walk into the city looking like I'd just fizzled there by some wormhole of style. But now I had a Russian haircut, I ate my apples with a jackknife, I scanned through Russian newspapers on the trolleys. No one queue-jumped me anymore either. Enough times I had verbally retaliated and left it understood what parts of the transgressor's anatomy would be ripped free and shown to the public. I still got looks of curiosity from the elderly. They scanned me head-to-toe. I always had my Canadian flag on my pack, so it wasn't my plot that thickened.

It is ironic that such a grey country like Russia is in love with colour. Everywhere there were gardens or attempts at urban horticulture. They sell flowers and plants at every other kiosk. Roses, daisies, daffodils. This was because (from someone who never really gave them much thought) flowers 'brighten up' the room. In a dismal Russian apartment - flowers 'live'. Cézanne, Monet, Renoir... I finally understood. Still, this country is Martha Stewart's Hell.

. . .

One night Sergei phoned, agitated. He was stumbling through his words and mixing his tenses. He had received a call from the American company that he hoped was going to hire him. This call from Colorado held his future in the balance. I calmed Sergei down and corrected his verbs.

'Sergei, what happened?' I asked. 'Did you convey a sensitivity to the fashioning of your past perfect? Did you express all of the subtle nuances towards the participles as we rehearsed? Not too many adjectives I hope...'

'?'

'Sorry, I've been lesson planning for two hours... Sergei?'

'... the man ask all questions, all questions we practiced.'

'Did you answer like we practiced?'

'I answered all like we did,' he said, breathing quickly.

'What did he say? Did you do well?'

'He said I am for sure good to come to America.'

'Are you going? Did they hire you?' I asked.

'I am sure yes. My papers must first to go to American Immigration.'

'But you did well right?' I said, 'You are going to be hired!'

'I am good and happy I should go to America... Brant?'

'Yes,' I replied.

'I zank you for being my teacher.'

I was so proud that I trembled. We were a success. I knew Sergei was proud of himself. Those goddamn tapes held their worth. We had worked many Sundays preparing for this and Sergei had done more alone. We had scripted telephone conversations and invented dialogue that might get used. It makes a tutor feel good when a student succeeds all the way from a sentence to a telephone interview.

. . .

Anya had to leave when my father came to visit. Anya had lived with me through February and into March. During this time, I learned that my father was going to visit me on an extended leg of a business trip to Germany. The plans fell together right and he would meet up with my brother and Hilary in Berlin, then carry on to Moscow where I would meet him.

The weeks Anya and I had shared were full of happiness and doom. I learned that, as much as I cared for Anya, I could never marry her. There was a fuse connected to her soul and I kept playing the part of a match. I am sarcastic when I am alone so a co-habitant is likely to bear some of that. I tried my best at accommodating her emotional needs but she was beyond my help. It was stressful being tied to someone as unstable as she was. Waking up to her every day, seeing her in class, and then having her get home before me was awkward.

It's not because she needs the TV volume at decibels that rattle my first-world fillings and it isn't the fact that she uses my toothbrush nor is it that old-person's snore she has, and it isn't even the fact I awoke to her whispering 'I love you. I kill you. But I love you forever'. Those were all the little things that, once added up, became big. There were no statistics, no pie charts or diagrams that I could draw for Anya to explain why I felt the way I did. So I translated some Nietzsche quotes to underline my feelings which in hindsight was a very, very wrong thing to do but it got across some important points. I still cared deeply for her. I just couldn't have her staying with me anymore. Her little prayers deserve answers. I'm just not one of them.

Igor knew of my pending trip to Moscow. He hinted several times at his accompanying me, how he'd like to visit Moscow and check out the nightlife. I hadn't picked up on it until he asked me outright. He asked to borrow a thousand rubles to join me. I was alarmed at first (for he had no real income to repay me) but I agreed and wore down the amount. I decided to provide him 600 rubles to follow along. It was a month's wage. I could have hired a bricklayer and built a wall somewhere. The deal was he would mention this to no one. He would sleep in the cheapest end of the train, and when we eventually were in Moscow, he would find somewhere else to stay. I had thwarted Sasha's hope of coming with me and had told Marina another time would best suit her. So no one knew that Igor, likely among the poorest of Voronezhians, was to accompany me to the great city. I took the money out of my account by using a new bank machine on the steps of a new bank and sheltered the bills as I flipped through them and handed the wad off to Igor. His eyes were quick and wide. The funds were a sacred bundle of potential. He tucked the money inside his jacket, zipped it closed, and we parted ways.

I left the Voronezh railway station on a late winter's night. Anya's wave left a lasting imprint on the train window as I slid away on the eve of Russia's second biggest holiday, Women's Day; bigger than Christmas, bigger than an election, as big as Russia herself. Anya had received a card and flowers from me. It was the wish of many people that I wasn't off to Moscow for the celebrations. I pressed my face to the train window and watched Anya, the platform, and the station all slide off.

I was just getting to know my own cabin's roommates when Igor walked by, obviously into vodka. He nodded in with his moppy hair and passed by the open door. I had stated emphatically that he couldn't interfere with any plans Dad and I made and that he would be left to fend for himself in terms of rooming and boarding. Any more time spent with him would likely result in further loans. He had agreed whole-heartedly and said we might just see one another in passing. Instead, Igor was running the length of the train looking for me. As I sat there wondering, he blurred by again. This time he stopped.

'Is you room yes?'

Igor had two hundred rubles left. He had dropped half of what I gave him on flowers for his mother.

'Is special flowers yes,' he said in his defence. 'Is special day yes.'

I was rooming with 47-year old Mikhail and 60-year-plus Boris. I watched the night seize Voronezh from the train and introduced myself. They were Education Ministers and I became the topic as they slurped on their vodka. Boris pushed me to share in their alcohol but I resisted. Turning down a drink for any reason is rude and offensive. It isn't easy *not* to drink in Russia. I was able to deflect the discussion and change the subject. My Russian had developed to where I was only then getting proud of my versatility. The choice to speak Russian or not had begun. Igor, being a student, had words to share with them. I dropped away from the discussion and watched as he let loose on the men for the education system and drank their vodka at the same time. The men were a good two generations from Igor and their views seemed to be rigid, linear, Soviet. The men would raise hands in drama and slap them on their trousers. Igor soon lost power and the old men, tired of holding up their shields against a young intellectual, decided to sleep. I looked to Igor so he'd leave, and closed the door.

A snowy Moscovian morning greeted me. So did rotten apples, halved and offered by Mikhail. Boris was timid and careful with his words; Mikhail was assertive and zealous. I listened to an hour of things Mikhail felt I should know about topics I wasn't familiar with in a dialect I didn't know. The train pulled into the station.

I met Igor at the end of the train. He'd booked tickets in the most economical part of the night train where 'sleeper' cars were substituted for seats. They were carriages of one noisy room with people on shelves. He was pale and his eyes were trying to focus. He had, he said with pride, been up all night. All these months of mini-communicating, of sliding around our languages and becoming comrades, I had forgotten that he was the age where irresponsibility, alcohol, and sleep deprivation are three of the four things you wake up for. We tackled the Metro for three stops in rush-hour's leading edge. It is quite literally like spawning. Oceans of people fight for foot space in a system built to be the best in the world - fifty years ago. Perhaps it was. But with multiple escalators under repair and places mysteriously cordoned off, age was defeating the Metro.

At the Rossiya Hotel, I confirmed my reservations for me and Dad but they'd been lost in Russian cyberspace. So I went through all the necessary booking information again and booked a room for later that evening.

On the edge of Red Square, Igor and I parted. He looked eager to hunt down a medicinal shot of vodka and then fill in the day and night with a hell of a party. He had the attitude that I once knew: that desire to just slip into a room with loud music, beautiful women and more alcohol than one could, however hard he tried, consume in a night. Igor gave me a thumbs-up at thirty paces and went off to the Russian underground.

I phoned Oleg, the man whose car I'd driven to the vodka picnic; the man whom I'd said I would smuggle into Canada. Oleg worked at the Duma, the Russian Federal parliament, for unlikely presidential candidate Vladimir Zhirinovsky. Oleg had said that if I ever made it to Moscow, I should look him up. I had forwarded him information stating my father was coming and that he was a leading tourism official in Canada. Oleg said possibly something could be done to correlate a meeting with senior members of the Liberal Democratic Party of Russia, or

LDPR as it is known. Oleg said, through the static, that there would be a tag at the Duma's security counter.

As I crossed Red Square, I was awed by the people on the roofs of the GUM State Department Store scraping off killer icicles. The city claims to have hired 25,000 novice climbers for the task because twenty to thirty people are killed each year by falling icicles. I was twice stopped by roving militsia asking for my passport and visa. I made my way to the door of the National Duma, failed a metal detector due to my lighter, and went to the 10th floor. Oleg had worked for the party for several years and handled many positions. Currently he was in charge of publicity and he handed off a full bag of pro-Zhirinovsky books, posters, magazines, CDs, and tapes then ushered me down to the cafeteria for lunch.

Dad had agreed to do a business engagement, if I thought it helpful. I made the connections and soon, thanks to Oleg and the LDPR, I sat myself in the rear of a black Duma Mercedes and headed to Sheremetyevo-2 airport to pick up Dad.

Dad's flight, titled 'Berlin-Hamburg' on the arrivals board, was frisked and released in colourful spurts of the 'other world'. Within a few seconds, Dad and I embraced in the same fashion as our first trip to the Soviet Union with Mom in 1974. I was a little taller than that five year old; Dad was a little greyer than that twenty-five year old. His speech was like I'd never known it before. He rattled off a blaze of English that knocked me back a step, then two. It was quick, laden with words like 'didja' and 'idunno' and his full freedom of structure.

Dad liked the Duma limousine, the Duma command of security in the foyer, the LDPR waiting room (a room laden with 800 pictures of Zhirinovsky) and the LDPR chai. Oleg let me phone and wake my mother up at 3am Vancouver time to wish her *S'vasmim 8th Marta*, Happy Women's Day, then Dad and I were led to a special boardroom where Oleg had arranged a meeting.

Zhirinovsky was out kissing ultra-leftist babies and instead of his participation, a meeting was held with Igor Shkryebyet-skij, Right-Hand Man (that is a literal translation from his Duma business card), Dmitry Gorshkov, Leading Specialist, and one other party member whose card later fell victim to a gust of wind in Red Square. Ideas were thrown about the room through a translator. A signed portrait of Saddam Hussein domi-nated a corner. I watched my Dad, trading off tourism facts and potential for Russia with the diplomacy of his career. When the meeting ended, Oleg was thanked for the opportunity. Dad and I left the Duma and walked through Red Square to visit my first McDonald's in six months. It was standing room only.

Dad checked his passport in at the Rossiya, 3300 rooms of ritual Soviet engineering. For forty dollars, we had a room two minutes away from St. Basil's Cathedral, the Kremlin, and GUM. Snow wove around us in the dusk and settled on the cobblestones of Red Square. Lenin was locked up for the holi-day. Just as we neared GUM and its late-19th century compo-sure on the eastern edge of the square, it was shut with a swiftness attributed only to bomb threats. Guards were waving their arms to the crowds at the exits and yelling 'SROCHNE POKIN'TE PEMISCHENIYE!!!'

'What are they saying?' Dad asked me.

'OUT! OUT! EVERYBODY GET THE FUCK OUT!!!' I said.

Police cars and fire trucks raced against the flow of shop-pers. In light of this inconvenience, we returned to the hotel room.

Dad unloaded stuff from home between sips of NeoCitran. One piece of luggage was a laptop. My Uncle Wayne had sent a little black Notebook that was far more powerful than the one I'd brought with me and I had anticipated it for weeks. I cradled the new computer on my knees in the bathroom where smoking was allowed but still frowned upon.

Dad and I awoke and laboured the luggage into a Volga taxi and parked everything at the Pavelyetskaya Station baggage check for our later departure. On the cool grey steps outside, in a snow shower, we plotted to sweep Moscow's high-traffic touristy areas for things that were not found in Voronezh, the Real Russia. The *Arbat* pedestrian street was five Metro stations away and twenty minutes later we were fending off Soviet scarves, matryoshki (nesting) dolls with Putin, gas masks, and packs of gypsy children.

Due to Women's Day, there were actually three days of holidays and this particular one was still observed so rigidly that both Dom Knigi (huge bookstore) and the Kremlin (huge red political triangle) were closed. As we neared five hours from our departure south, we sat in the Rossiya bar and mused about the 1974 trip to Russia and the Ukraine, many stories from our Trans-Siberian train trip in 1997, and I enlightened Dad on what he could expect in Voronezh. Then we called a cab and made our way to the station.

We boarded to a pleasant surprise despite the crushing hoard of fellow train travellers. The two of us were entirely alone in a second-class coach with a *providnitsa*[1] named Olga who was none-too-happy that she had two Canadians who emptied their own garbage and straightened the vestibule mats. The third-class was packed floor to ceiling with people.

Voronezh pulled alongside the curtained train windows at eight a.m. Sasha was standing on the platform with SashaZ and Oxana. Dad had agreed to baptize Voronezh with the wisdoms of tourism and destination-marketing. SashaZ had tracked down Oxana, who was able to help us secure meetings with Voronezh's travel and tourism people for the province. We piled everything into Oxana's Audi 100 and sped off to my flat. Dad

---

1. Carriage attendant

was overwhelmed at the time and dedication that went into the preparation for his arrival. Anya had cleaned every single thing twice the day before, and then disappeared. The five of us sipped on chai until Oxana said it was time for my driving test. I would take her to work and if we survived that, I had her car for the day.

An Audi in Voronezh is like a Ferrari in Medicine Hat; rare and respected. Six months of pedestrianism had dunced a lot of my driving habits but Oxana praised my double-helixing of the traffic and missed seeing me run an amber light. As she stepped out of the car, SashaZ climbed into the seat beside me. The two of us wound out third gear down Prospect Revolution. Oxana's cell phone rang from under the seat and, concluding she'd forgotten it, I pulled a perfect U-turn across four lanes. A whistle, a baton, a cop pulled us over to the side. SashaZ laughed, said it was his buddy from the village and he left to talk us out of whatever extortion fees I had to pay.

After returning the phone and letting SashaZ off at his place, I chuckled to myself that I was alone and driving in the city I only knew on foot. As I crossed Plexhanovskaya Street at an alleged 78 kilometres per hour, twelve militsia waving batons pulled me over. I stepped from the car at gun point and was placed in the rear of a police car. I began to calculate how much it would cost to pay them all off as the interviewing officer winced at my choppy Russian. My paperwork, vehicle registration, and a permission note from Oxana were scrutinized. And I was released.

Dad had started cleaning things even Russians don't clean. Marina soon showed up. I had expressly granted her all interpreting rights for Dad's visit. Her command of English, along with hours searching tourism-related web sites, was ready for anything Dad might try to communicate to someone else. Marina was gold.

A meeting was held with the Institute's president, Yuli Zolotovinski – my big boss. 'Bridges between countries' were constructed in the air. The recent stresses between Russia and America, from spies to aid cutbacks to missile shields, were all reasons to be thankful of my citizenship. Canada stood up to the meeting and laughs were freely exchanged. My employer offered a Sunday afternoon meeting and lunch. Dad was happy with that.

Marina, Dad, and I walked back to my place and set off in the car for a tour of Voronezh. Marina guided us down the hill, through the shacks and wrecked streets, to the riverbank church. Having survived a war that destroyed 96% of Voronezh, the *Ospinskaya* church was worth seeing before it sinks further into the ground. We walked through Victory Square, drove to the Church of the Shroud, and raced a tram. I mused that I could outrun any Lada cop car in the city. Not that I knew my way anywhere but just the thought was worthwhile.

'We could make Kazakhstan by midnight...' I said.

Marina was defiant. 'Even if every paper was in order, we would be extorted blindly,' she said, referring to the many road checks we'd encounter.

'We could throw a 'Drive for Christ' sign on the roof or something...' I suggested.

Dad sided with Marina. I dropped the car back with Oxana as he entertained Lucia at my apartment, then Igor, and gave the drunk next door a Euro and twenty-six pence. After encouraging everyone to leave politely so I could have a while to myself with this man 'who smells like burning leaves' (as Igor described the pipe smoker), Dad and I were alone.

We went across the street to the Rossiya State Department Store. Dad couldn't understand why salt and pepper were on opposite sides of the state food department. He bought six suspicious meat pies, a month's supply of *Kalicheevski* cheese, and Byelorussian two-ply toilet paper. He got himself a trench coat and bought me a Russian cap. We dropped three months Russian salary in twenty-six minutes, bought utensils for purposes I can't figure out and got more dented fruit than my flat had seen. Dad also bought a cheap touch-tone phone to replace my rotary.

We spent the night doing tag-team emails home and checking voice messages. I also called Mom since the Duma call had been quick and early. But in the clearness of the Russian phone lines, I felt like she was no further than Warsaw. My eyes welled as she put Shasta's little doggie nose to the receiver. It beeped.

I had forgotten how loudly Dad snores. I let him use my personal room, my bed, and had even shut him away from me for the night. But the snoring was incessant and foreboding, living in the walls. The young girl next door who cries through the wall at night must have been screaming. It lasted until he woke early and got dressed in a racket. I knew he was going out for a walk. Dad likes to explore a new city before anyone is up. He wrapped himself up snug and pressed himself into the living room.

'You're up early,' I said winding an eye with my fist.

'I didn't sleep as well as I could have. That bed has a funny bow in it,' Dad said.

'It's Russian… if something doesn't have some odd peculiarity to it that means it's imported.'

'I see. Well, I thought I'd go and smell the city. I won't wander long… wanna come?' Dad asked.

'No. I've done that tour often. Are you going far enough that I'll have to get dressed and look for you?'

'A couple of streets, squares and maybe duck into a restaurant for breakfast.'

'Ha. Breakfast starts at eleven here. You'll only find the odd kiosk open.' Then I stepped gingerly towards the precipice. 'Don't fret over the meal. Anya is coming by to cook something.' I hesitated. 'Whatta girl eh?'

'Yeah, how do you know her?'

'She's a third year,' I said.

'You're dating a student?'

'Easy... don't go Canadian on me. She's older than Mom and you were when you got married...' He eyed me with parental suspicion. 'And it's different here. The vice-president of the school's 57 and he's marrying the 24 year old receptionist. Mistresses, multiple girlfriends...'

'I see. Well it's not like she's *living* here,' he said.

We both laughed.

Dad, SashaZ, Marina, and I later piled into Oxana's small Audi. Oxana drove us through a frosty neighbourhood on Voronezh's outskirts. The high apartment buildings were set in snow and the thin trees were leafless. She found a side street. There was a row of mismatched houses and Oxana pulled off the dirt road into a paved driveway. The home was small and had a small yard. Oxana said this was the finest *banya*, or sauna in Voronezh. Ivan, the owner and proprietor, stepped down his front steps into the snow in slippers. Ivan had a broad nose that ended in a Stalin-esque moustache. He gripped a snow shovel like it was a battle axe. A small hunter's hat sat on his unkempt hair. He was amusing, punctuated by mirth-filled high cheeks. He took us around the side of his house to the backyard where a small shack held the *banya*. A few stepping stones away sat a swimming pool. The top of it was frozen thick and covered with snow. A small hole six square feet had recently been cut out of the ice, exposing frigid water.

Only Dad, SashaZ, and I were to endure the punishing banya. Oxana and Marina opted for sweet tea inside with Ivan. Just inside the banya, Dad and SashaZ took off their shirts and pants and I began to follow. Then SashaZ continued until he was naked. Then Dad. There is a mental bruising that takes place when you see your father nude. I winced. And I winced again when my own underwear hit the floor. And to top it all off, SashaZ was gay.

We opened a narrow door and walked into the sauna. Ivan had fired it up earlier and it was hot. Then it was hotter. The rocks steamed and the air lost oxygen. The cedar benches were stupidly uncomfortable. As the temperature grew to where it could grow no more, SashaZ leapt to a corner and grabbed a handful of birch branches, replete with leaves and edges, and probably bugs. He proceeded to slap, whack, strike, beat, and smack Dad's back, then he moved to me. This is customary, and many may call it refreshing but it was lost on me. Dad and I lay on scalding benches, being assaulted by a naked man. SashaZ said it was time for his slapping and he handed me the bushel. I whacked SashaZ and he cried for more, harder. I thrashed him a good minute or two before putting my arm out. I was covered in sweat; it ran off my body in tiny beads.

'Enough!' yelled SashaZ 'To the pool!'

We ran nude from a hundred and thirty degree heat straight outside, barefoot through the snow, and jumped into the freezing cold water. Marina, Oxana, and Ivan looked on. It was nearly pleasant for a brief few seconds then it grew *very* cold.

'Enough!' yelled SashaZ 'Back to the banya!'

We did this crazy run between the two climes a couple of times. You barely had time to shiver before leaping into the infernal heat. Each time we were out of doors, Marina, Oxana, and Ivan cheered. I couldn't tell which part of this process the

Russians loved but it was a strange way to welcome a foreigner. I think alcohol is required to add anything positive to the event, a lot of alcohol. Dad was the first to leave and settle in the tiny room where we'd disrobed. I told SashaZ that I'd had all the fun I could have, and that now I was entering the realm of agitated and disturbed. He begged for a few more slaps of the twigs and I obliged. Then I exited and sat down nude with Dad. There was a table and a few benches. Ivan came in to stoke the fireplace, heated borscht, and brewed tea.

When we were dressed, Ivan toured us around his place. He was a hobby-geneticist and had spliced green plants with purple plants; had joined blue plants with red ones. I failed to see all the wonder in his exploits. He had hundreds of little plants growing in a greenhouse. I could think of a better use for his hydroponics room than merging colourful shoots. I knew SashaZ was thinking the same thing.

After loading into the car to leave, Oxana waved while backing up. This landed the car in a ditch. Everyone got out and looked at the damage. Oxana was prone to slips of this nature, and shrugged. Ivan came out and helped us look at the situation. I packed a tight snowball, recoiled and sent it at Marina. She looked as though she'd taken a bullet. She reached down, scooped up some snow and tossed it at SashaZ. SashaZ, who had been grunting at the car, trying to shift the weight this way or that, grabbed a mitfull of snow. I launched a pre-emptive strike against Dad and he in turn went for me but got Marina. I knew that sooner or later Oxana would get knocked off her high heels so I threw lightly at her. It looked like she'd been taken down by a pack of huskies. She shrieked and crawled behind Ivan for cover. But Ivan was packing a Russian snowball for SashaZ For a splinter of childish time, we ran around the car, ducking and weaving snowballs, laughing and screaming. Soon, though, someone got hit hard in the face and we had to stop.

The four men lifted the car back onto the road and we all waved at Ivan while leaving his banya, *the finest in Voronezh.*

Oxana pulled her car into the small horseshoe of road behind my apartment. Dad, Marina, and I had a dinner date at the Institute. A mild chill hung in the air. Dad and Marina were getting along famously. Marina erupted with a whole fresh linguistical conduct. She was used to teaching English through slow, methodical classes. With Dad and me, she spoke English with freedom and autonomy. Dad loved talking with Marina and Marina loved him back. We walked through the snow to the Institute – friends all.

Valeri and Sasha were in the office, typing madly away on their respective computers. We ordered pizza from the only delivery service in the city of one million. The pizza was a respectable facsimile of anything found in North America. It was at this point I began to get a horrible feeling in my stomach. By the time the pizzas arrived I was too unwell to participate in the feast. Instead I left Dad among my peers and slowly walked home for a bath. As I climbed into bed, I could hardly stand.

I awoke the next morning definitely a bit sick but I could walk, talk, and smoke, all the essentials. Dad was sleeping like he'd been tranquilized. I was puzzled at my illness. It was the same as the night before, only diminished. It was a deep and penetrating pain in my entire lower torso. When Dad got up and was finished complaining about the smoke that hung in the air, he asked how I was feeling. I told him my symptoms and said I was getting better.

Oxana had lined up an interview with two brothers, two of the richest men in Voronezh. The plan had been that when she arrived, we would go and pick up Marina. Marina was our translator, something she had earned. Dad favoured Marina whole-heartedly and it was quite a shock when Oxana drove up with SashaZ in the passengers' seat. As we climbed in and headed off to the suburbs, Dad asked about Marina and was told that Oxana preferred SashaZ as interpreter. I liked SashaZ but this change in plans was cruel and inappropriate. Marina deserved the spotlight, the chance to show her competence. As we drove on, the car fell silent. Oxana, we would learn, had a 'thing' for SashaZ. As well, it wasn't uncommon for a woman to prefer men over women as translators.

At the restaurant, which was owned by the two brothers, we were welcomed by courteous staff who had obviously been directed to provide us the finest of customer service. This was strange because customer service is an attribute of business sense that Russia hasn't perfected. Here, however, in the upscale café, we were given the finest treatment. It soon became obvious the entire restaurant was closed for the privacy of our meeting. It was a testament to the influence that Dad commanded, or they thought he did. The room was warm and inviting. There was a dance floor and a karaoke machine. The staff offered tea, juice, and beer before the brothers came and sat with us. They felt powerful, their presence formed of deep voices and wide shoulders. As we ordered, they pressed Dad on how hotels in the western world generate their revenue. It was their intention to tear down a few of the old structures on the most expensive property on Prospect Revolution and build their interpretation of a five star hotel. There wasn't a hotel in the city beyond one star. These sad hotels seldom had running water, lacked sufficient toilets, and were crawling with cock-roaches. They were, in effect, like my flat. But Dad was full of promise, detailing the obstacles they may face. Through a satis-fying lunch of soups, salads, fish, fowl, and feathers, the table of people brainstormed the prospects of various ventures.

Oxana was silent, beautifully dressed and politely spooning caviar onto her plate. SashaZ was handsomely suited with a bright tie. He was wisely using his hands to translate the topics. I didn't mind SashaZ doing the interpretation after all, for he was dashing in a certain way. I sat there letting the clock run out. I had little to contribute to the discussion, and besides, I had my increasing pain to contend with. I was rather amazed at Dad's control of the situation, his knowledge, his honesty, and his own presence.

We left the brothers who seemed pleased with their time with Dad. Some of their ideas had been shot down but others had been given the boost they needed. We drove on and soon parked on Prospect Revolution. Oxana had arranged a meeting with Viktor, the Director of Tourism for the Voronezh province. We seated ourselves in an office lined with mostly empty book-shelves. The secretary delivered tea and we waited. Viktor approached. He was elderly, dressed loosely in a suit, and hobbled towards us. As SashaZ began translating, I could tell that Viktor had no insights to offer. This, the director of tourism, was poorly educated in matters pertaining to tourism. His post, I quickly guessed, was merely maintained in order to validate its existence and provide a job. He learned a lot from Dad's chatter. But Dad didn't take away much from him. The meeting lasted two cups of tea, and we left.

I was feeling progressively unwell but I didn't let on to Dad. It felt the kind of serious that would have me on a plane against my will. I didn't want any talk of me going home. Dad and I got dropped off at my flat and thanked Oxana and SashaZ

Inside my apartment Anya and Nona were making a grand Russian dinner. Many people wanted some of Dad's time and we had to keep his schedule hushed. Anya had pleaded for the opportunity to serve Dad local cuisine before our return train's departure to Moscow. The girls were dressed in their finest. The apartment was clean and the garbage cans were emptied. It had all the trademarks of Anya cooking dinner. She was cute and courteous, almost refined. I never saw her acting as precious as I did that night.

Lucia was there, as Lucia always seemed to be. She tried to make an Italian dish but got fed up with the Russian pasta and flushed it down the toilet. Instead, she baked bread. We feasted on Anya's gifted dumplings and sipped grape juice. The meal was topped off with sugar pancakes that Nona had oh-so perfected.

The time came when Dad and I had to shoulder our bags and set off to the train station. Valeri screeched his car to a stop, apologized for being late, and took Dad and his belongings through a last look at the city. I went with Anya and Nona on the tram reserved for the lower forms of Russian life. The trams were noisy and filled with drafts; they dragged sparks along the wires and their lights flickered. They were loud and cold, and one was compelled to hate travel on them. And from hate, one can discern love. Since I was a foreigner, I could tell the difference, and I preferred the authentic Russian experience.

We made it to the train station as my father and Valeri were carrying his things through the tall gate to the platform. My stomach ached and I walked slowly with the girls. It was 7:20pm and our train was due to arrive momentarily. Dad spoke gaily about Voronezh and thanked everyone for their part in my life, for their hospitality and the chance to spread good tourism vibes. The train rocked into the lane and our wagon stopped just short of us. We smiled as the *providnitsa* confirmed our tickets and we rose up the steps. Lucia was smiling her Italian smile. Anya and Nona were doing short, limited palm waves. It was all so perfect.

Our train arrived in the morning. Moscow with Dad has been fun before on three previous trips. He is great to wander a city with, and rarely complains about aches. He never says 'how much further' and he seldom displays any wishes of wanting to be elsewhere; he is wonderful to be out and about with.

We checked him back into the Hotel Rossiya where he would spend this night alone. I was getting sicker and decided on a change of plans. I would be on the southbound train back to Voronezh. We crossed Red Square in the fresh and vibrant sunshine. It was late winter and the city was in the last of its icings. The domes of Saint Basils gleamed with frost and GUM looked every bit the old building it should. Crossing the square, we made an early lunch at a pizza place in the Manezh Square mall just off the concourse of the Kremlin. Happily fed, Dad and I marched along back streets towards the Arbat, the pedestrian street. Moscow wove around us. In this Moscow of timelessness, the buildings and lanes we walked were silent and hidden from the fast-paced traffic, both foot and vehicle. We owned these snowy streets. Father and son laughed and talked in the coolness of the day.

We went to the *Dom Knigi,* the finest bookstore on the Novy Arbat. It was a mess of children's toys, videos, maps, flags, stationery, and books. Dad spent an hour scouring for gifts to take home. Lazily, we crossed over to the true Arbat, the touristy street relegated to foot-traffic. The vendors were well into their day - carts, their sellers on stools, displayed their wares. Everything from T-shirts to art, musicians to CCCP trinkets, was for sale by someone who had a loose grip on English. Snow sat in pockets of shade. Where the sun could penetrate, steam poured from the street.

Dad and I parted at Red Square. I slowly climbed into the back of a Lada taxi. My eyes welled. I have left my parents many times before but this was exceptional, this was worth tears. They were not tears of sadness but of pride that my father had made it to my small city, where I lived, and I was leaving him in a magical city. As he shut the car door and the taxi sped into traffic, I winced at the pain that I'd kept from him. I was now bound for Pavelyetskaya Station and my return to Voronezh. Dad had the night in the Rossiya Hotel, a planned nostalgic dinner at the stately Hotel Metropol (where we had stayed 26 years before). Then, early in the morning, he would return to Canada.

When I was five years old, I was taken to see the movie *Doctor Zhivago* by parents who didn't have a copy of Doctor Spock. While Dad was in Voronezh, 'Doctor Toboggan' reared its ugly head again. Dad merrily told the story of my speech impediment over *Zhivago* at the malleable age of five and my current friends thought it cute. But it was now personal, Zhivago is a variation of *zheet*, Russian for the verb *to live*.

I no longer refer to the USSR as the Soviet Onion, and, as for Zhivago, I can now pronounce it so scorchingly Russian that people can't tell I'm Canadian. I'm that good. It is now my moniker, alias and password. I am Zhivago.

A Russian Spring

Spring pulled a surprising punch and ended winter in the space of a day. At once, it seemed, leaves had been thrown on the trees, birds belted into song, and the populace lost their heavy coats. Winter snuck off to the fields into the forests and slid along the icy Don. My view out the living room windows, which had been the majestic Rossiya department store, was obscured by full trees and budding branches. Everyone rejoiced in the warmth of the sun and praised the blue sky. There were smiles and giggles on the lips of all these female Voronezhians. They were invigorated, challenging, dressed in miniskirts and bounding up stairs to their classes. Workers whistled while they whittled their bricks, and outdoor cafes righted their tables and chairs.

I made a discovery that struck fear into my heart. My stomach seemed severe, terminal, as though all my hypochondria had paid off. I was hobbling to school. In time I knew I'd be calling Marina for medical assistance. I had tried to wait out the pain, convinced that enduring it would eventually lead back to good health. But then I found it, something that dismissed any doubt I was still all right. A testicle had doubled in size. How had I missed this? I just never really put my attention to it. Maybe I don't fidget with the status quo. Everything in my nether region ached. I didn't need to search for any more clues or evidence. Now I was facing something I'd never encountered: going home because of a medical emergency. I sat alone in my flat and drew conclusions that only a desperate man can draw. I made excuses, I avoided the issues, and I sat in dread. It was doubt consolidation. Only after I'd exhausted myself with thoughts about 'you musta take ze next big plane ride home', only then did I call Marina.

'You idiot!' she said, 'You've endured this for how long?'

'Since we went to the banya…'

'Men,' she coughed.

'Yes,' I said, 'The entire gender is messed up. We don't go to the doctor unless we are dying, dead, or something is happening down south.'

'Wait there. I'll phone my mother and we'll get you in to get checked out. I'm sure it's nothing serious.'

'From my vantage point, stuck in a rusty scalpel, bring-your-own-anesthesia country like Russia, it is serious.'

'Wait there you fool… Men.'

'They're gonna FedEx my ass home.'

'Wait there.'

Marina got me an appointment for the following day. She had my classes covered. Anya called from Nona's and I told her that I had a horribly disfiguring cough and that I would see her in a few days time. The day recessed into a lonely and pitiful darkness. I smoked through a package of cigarettes in the dark. The night and I were not friends. I got on the computer and wrote an autobiography in twenty-seven minutes and emailed it to Penguin Classics. I flipped in bed, ever so carefully. The pain was intense and nothing alleviated it. A Russian doctor… a Russian diagnosis… Russia has a socialistic health care system and every Russian is covered for basic medical care. However, since there is little money for the hospitals, or the nurses and doctors, patients are often required to buy things like their own anesthesia. Marina had sinus surgery and had to save a half month's pay to 'go under'. Most Russians can't afford the medication and forfeit themselves to excruciating pain or, yes, alcohol. No, the night was not kind; there wasn't a pleasant thought to be had. When Marina showed up at my door in the morning, I couldn't help but hold her tight.

'Why did you wait to tell me this?' she asked.

'I figured if it didn't kill me, it would only make me stronger…'

'Did you think that maybe it *is* killing you?'

'I thought I was getting stronger. I'm an optimist Marina. All Canadians are.'

'You are a fool Mister Antonson.'

'I think I gave myself an ulcer being so optimistic.'

'There is a Russian proverb…'

'Don't you dare… this is not proverb territory.'

I shuffled down the stairs and out into the day. We hailed a car and made our way across town. As we pulled up to the doctor's office, I nearly had the driver turn around and head for the train station. The building which housed the offices looked blown apart. There were bricks scattered around the yard and the walls were teetering on collapse. A minority of windows were intact. Steel poked from the roofline and hung over a crowd of elderly pensioners waiting at the door. I expected to see many fire trucks arriving to check in on the incident. There were craters in the ground between the old people in queue,

scarring craters like someone had been digging graves for a
month. No serious doctor would hold his practice in this
decrepit hole in the earth, I thought. He's got to be a quack,
lowest grades in his class. But, I reasoned, I had the lowest
grades in my class and I'm not a quack. But then – what if he
skipped classes too? Oh God… I squeezed my jacket pocket
and felt the few imported needles I had with me. For Marina, it
was all second-nature and she was not phased by this display of
horrific first impressions. She pulled me from the car and past
the long line of elderly people. I was shuffling slower than
them. The stairs were losing a battle against time. The railing
came off in my hand and the door fell open on its last hinge. I
was sure that I would walk out of the building one testicle
lighter.

The doctor was a jovial old guy with a knack for making the
best of his situation. In fact to watch him, you could see there
was no situation. He was in his fifties and had a hunk of white
hair combed across his forehead. He wore a white smock which
gave him status until I remembered coroners wear them too.
There were dusty books lining the cracked plaster on the walls.
The doctor was proud of his new desk and I watched as he and
Marina rattled off a few knocks on it. My imminent death had
taken backseat to a desk; warning sign. Marina described my
symptoms and the good doctor looked at me with compassion,
furrowing his eyebrows in thought. Then he rapped his
knuckles on the desk and looked to see if its legs were plumb.
Marina continued talking. The doctor waved me over and asked
me to undo my pants.

'Painful to walk?' Marina translated his question.

'Yes… it is painful to walk,' I replied.

'How is your stool?' he asked through Marina.

'… the stool is fine.'

'Poop?' he turned to me.

'*Da, da*' I said, 'Poop *harisho.*'

'Do you have trouble getting an erection?' Marina asked.

'Only when I'm around you.'

'How is your sleep?' she queried.

'I can get by on two hours…'

'Two hours a night?'

'Yeah what bothers me is the six hours it takes me to get to sleep. I dare say it has to do with the flat and its twenty metre proximity to the 24 hour transit.'

Then, with probing fingers and thumbs, he worked his way around my not-so-private privates. There was a mixed professionalism in the whole procedure. He pulled, twisted and squeezed. His opinion was addressed to Marina and she nodded in the affirmative.

'You are alright Brant… it is nothing serious, the doctor will give you medicine.' she said. 'Five injections into the testicle each day for a month then return to see him.'

I dropped my pants in horror. My belt buckle made a lonely clink as it hit the floor. Then they broke into a laughing fit. 'No, the doctor was kidding, oral medicine, makes you sleepy.'

The doctor lit up a cigarette and passed the pack around. After zipping up and dropping some rubles on the nice desk, Marina scolded me. It turned out that the banya, what with all its zipping back and forth to extremes (which had seemed like a really stupid idea anyway), was responsible for swelling me up. There were antibiotics to be taken, and I was to abstain from all manner of professional sports and rest. I wasn't going home on the next flight out. And that was all that mattered to me. I was indebted to Marina. She had come through once again. I begged her to keep this medical piece of my life out of the grapevine but somehow I knew that everyone would know in time. Gossip was bigger than the self. Hell, the doctor will probably have it on his blog by dinner.

The antibiotics worked fast and I was chided over and over again by Marina for not dealing with the situation earlier. I was still her responsibility. If I screwed anything up, it was Marina who was dealt the blow by the school's administration. But with the rejuvenation inherent in a receding illness, I felt bulletproof and potent. My life ballooned into an appreciation for my situation. I challenged my classes with new insights. My time in Voronezh, which had seemed to be at an end, was again valuable, dear and extended. The fair weather contributed too. The winter had been nasty and encompassing. With the coming of spring came activity. There were V-Day holidays and communist parades. There were picnics, strolls through rail yards, and walks in the forest. There were bumblebees and daydreams. The old fountain in the park even came to life for a few minutes. The pensioners on Plexhanovskaya tore the tarpaulins off their heirlooms. Flowers, in such abundance, were selling out at all of the kiosks. Birds took to the skies overhead and old women with twig brooms began sweeping up the sandings that had been spread over the roads. Everything was again wonderful and I was living on the edge of my surfboard. Spring was a magical moment in a time called Russia.

Russia hasn't had much 'positive exposure' for nine hundred years. It has been torn apart by credible news agencies as long as there have been news agencies. Many people have been misled to believe that Russian stores are still the way they used to be. Under the final sigh of Communism, there were queues for bread, milk, and cheese that stretched for entire days. Trying to buy luxury items was next to impossible. And often the list of luxury items included bread, milk, and cheese. But all that had changed and rather emphatically at that. Now the stores were brimming with goods, both domestic and foreign. Some of the longest queues were at the lottery booths. There were wide varieties of fresh, canned, wholesale, or baked commodities. A trip into a supermarket 'post-communism' was an adventure that only got better by the day. There was an assortment of distilled spirits but they aren't all Russian and they aren't all vodka. You can get fine Georgian wines, Czech brandies, and Irish whiskey. There were juices, fruits, and imported dates. It was no longer a tricky task to collect ingredients for supper. However, there was still a very Russian way about *buying* what you want. For all the freedom Russia has learnt to play with, purchasing was still a missed opportunity at improvement. One fault was the tiered system for foreigners.

It goes something like this: '*Ezveni, do you have um, -*'

The counter girl reached down and produced two packages, both above-the-honest-Russian's-financial-grasp. One was 295 rubles and the other package of 4 was 250 rubles.

'Don't you have anything cheaper?' I said in Russian with a smirk implying I knew she did. She assumed by my Russian accent that I was a rich foreigner wanting expensive foreign brands. She reached over to the other display and laid down a pack of 12. Then she tapped it.

I asked 'How much, *skolka stoit?'*

'*12 rublay.*' she said harbouring a 'tsk-tsk' under her moustache.

'Ha, *harisho,*' I said and reached for my change. Now I was given a chit, a small piece of paper that said '12 rublay - latex'. After I paid a cashier, received another chit, I then walked back to the girl in front of the Trojan display and got my purchase. Throughout Russia, this line-up to line-up to line-up tradition continues. In this example, after a half hour of bullshit, I got twelve condoms for twelve rubles. Although I wasn't buying quality at that price….

. . .

My Russian advanced unpredictably. I could say a lot of things in the present. I imagine it is quite interesting for listeners/sympathizers to hear me tell a story in shifting tenses. I thought I'd proven to Voronezh that I was not a spy. No civil country would stick someone waving his Russian about like me.

Questions had been asked indirectly, in fact, about me being a spy ('shpeon' in Russian). Even my best friends had suspected me. Binoculars? Laptop? Portable CD player? Buys a whopping eight CDs at a time? Develops every picture? Takes to his pipe and shoulders the cold to walk into the bad part of town? Does he even know it's the bad part of town? If so, how? And he has seventeen toothbrushes and forty little soaps from a Canadian airline. Why is that? We get one toothbrush a year if we're lucky. He takes pictures of hammers and sickles? He does British, Iranian, and American accents? He needed to see Lenin Square in the blizzard? He takes Karl Marx street to the university... he bought Russian boots... therefore Russian footprints. He spends ten minutes flushing... says he enjoys yanking our chain. What is up with that behavior? Did anyone actually read his resume? If he is a spy, perhaps it is just personal. Canada could do better.

As per Russian tradition, my most recent paycheque had been at the end of January; the next has been projected and promised for late April. One day there just wasn't a paycheque or a reason. I truly felt the Russian predicament when my paycheques stopped coming. That meant I had to call home for a money transfer and that in turn meant I'd have less money when I returned home. My father was guarding my dwindling financial reserves and applying what I needed to my credit card for ease of access. That new instant teller machine broke one day and was not repaired, forcing me back to banks. I hated using the card. Not because of the money but because the idea was still so foreign to the average bank. A credit card was an advanced science. It could take four to six bank staff a half hour to process a transaction. Therefore, a cash withdrawal was only done when it was absolutely needed. Here is my point: I make twelve times what a secretary earns. I am hungry. My Dad filled my flat with stuff I'll never be able to eat. But I do have food and money; hunger is just something I enjoy more than most people. Conversely, my co-workers are hungry, their families are hungry and for them, going without a paycheque can be cruel. Going without two is life-threatening. Never mind the angst and the postponements given the landlord, going without money is a personal implosion. And this is characteristic of Russia. And it doesn't matter how employed you are, paycheques are missing from every sector of society.

It was Easter. In the market there were coloured eggs and dead rabbits. I walked alone to the Church of the Shroud as the sun slipped from the sky. Both Lucia and Natasha were there and they were sporting headscarves and crossing themselves. Hundreds of Russians converged inside the church and spilled out the doors. There were long rows of tables with homemade cakes awaiting an Easter blessing. I walked around and looked at the crowd of old people and young couples. There were two pesky gypsy children trying to separate me and my wallet. The boy and his sister were dressed in ragged clothes and they found my camera a source of amazement. I tempted them into posing for a photo with an American dollar bill. This boy was no more than nine or ten years old and he was halfway through a cigarette as I snapped off a few pictures and gave them an extra dollar bill. Natasha told me not to encourage them with money or they would come back with all their friends, brothers, and sisters. I told her not to be silly. They left and arrived swiftly with all their friends, brothers, and a few sisters. An aunt hobbled to Lucia and muttered a gypsy curse on her after she refused to give up any money. Natasha spoke in a slicing reprimand and the aunt cowered and swept away the children. I walked out back of the church and lit my pipe. A handful of clergy were there smoking their cheap Russian cigarettes and bitching about how hot they were under their cassocks and robes.

Lucia and I squeezed into the church and watched the service but it was full and the babushkas owned the floor. The night was interrupted by a thousand candles as the priest led a procession outside. The priest, accompanied by a holy-water-boy who carried a bucket, ritually began dousing the tiny cakes with a splash of H-H2O and a monotone prayer. I interrupted him between cakes and asked if I could take his picture. His pupils dilated and the old woman who owned the next cake gasped.

'Why?' he said, 'Jesus Christ, why on Earth do you want to capture this moment and blessings on film? God Almighty! Isn't it good enough just to watch?'

I shrank and withdrew a step, encouraging him to just go about his duties and forget that I had ever been conceived. Lucia was nowhere to be found, there was no one on my side. The insulted priest gave me a long three second glance of utter disgust and then turned to the babushka's lopsided cake. As he raised his hands in devotion, I stepped in and lit up the priest with my camera's flash. If I was going to ruin his Easter, I wanted to remember it.

My laptop developed a strange and foreign disease. It died, taking with it all of my writings. I had spent the better part of three hours a night, each night, writing and lesson planning and throughout that time I trusted the Russian world outside that thieves would not enter my second-story apartment. I trusted people with keys to that apartment. I trusted students and friends with the computer and the apartment. And I had been the one to destroy it.

I found that most of what I downloaded was stuff to make the computer happier. And I had used up every last byte of memory before it knew what hit it. It seemed that there was a hard-drive crisis and during one writing session, a horrible noise, one that seemed to involve everything inside, whirred and stopped all processing. My eyes were wide as I watched for life. It made a pitiful noise, a guttural gagging. 'A man's not supposed to out-live his computer,' I wept. I cried as one burying his dead. I say this truthfully because the contents of my computer were like a child to me. I have worked, trained, and learnt on my computer. I taught it Windows, it taught me DOS. There were three manuscripts in the gut of it and all of the meaning for many years of my written life. Without all of that information, I ceased to exist in all but the physical sense.

I left the computer with the technicians at the Institute and praised them for taking on the task when no one had been paid in months. I trusted them and the thing is, that I had just left all of my personal information to them. I had visions of the FSB being called in and rooms of various-level people decoding my life. You see, I had a manuscript which was all about travelling the Trans-Siberian railway. There wasn't anything overly incriminating in it but some of the text wasn't Russia-friendly. I had sworn not to bring it to Russia just in case it fell in front of the wrong eyes. Well, I had downloaded it from a cyberspace account so I could change a few items that I'd since learned were different. Add to that my alien encounter and some pictures of people and things and people with things, writers were exiled for less….

I was without my laptop for two weeks. A computer crash to the computer-illiterate seems a strange, benign, and harmless event. But it can be devastating and make one do things they'd normally not do. I, for one, read three books, drew fourteen pictures, cleaned behind the toilet, and visited the opera twice. Since I couldn't surf the internet, I moved my magnetic alphabet around the fridge and spelt words. Instead of signing on at night and greeting my family as they got to work, I tended to cobwebs, stood in longer lines, and learned to pick a lot of stuff up with my toes. Instead of tapping away thoughts into the keyboard, I bought a quill made in Kyrgyzstan, but acquired on Plexhanovskaya, and resigned myself to parchment. When my laptop was returned, it had been formatted. Everything had been erased. In doing this, the problem had been corrected. I, however, would never really recover.

From the Institute's third computer, I moaned at length in one email to my Dad. He said that he had older copies of my manuscripts and I should move on and depend less on machines that could have been stolen or seized anytime in the last six months anyway.

I came to understand my foolishness. I was at that time one of very few people with a personal computer in Voronezh. And I was part of a far smaller number of people with access to the internet. And still I was part of an elite group of those who had a laptop. I swore never again to let myself become a slave to my computer. My time in Russia, each long second, was a chance to enjoy Voronezh and the life I was living.

I went to the local software dealers on the curb, cross-examined the plywood stands and walked away with $3000 in software for twelve American dollars. The Russian pirates sail to the farthest shores of Microsoft, Electronic Arts, Sierra, Sony, Adobe, Nintendo, the latest-translated DVDs et al. Nothing is sacred. This was one of the reasons it was so hard to get good businesses to come to the former Soviet Union. Investment money goes into the shadow economy and reappears as a 'New Russian' who suddenly likes imported cigarettes, monogrammed socks, and atriums. Products and services, rich and poor, have and have-nots, supply and demand - there is a multiplication table using these which tells you your status, where you fit in the country. The ghost of the Iron Curtain is economic and still a barrier of dreams. This is the deathbed of communism, the 21st century Russia… where you can buy Coke in a Pepsi machine.

SashaZ and I were walking alongside the Voronezh Duma when he asked me if I'd like to meet his friends who were in town from Moscow. They were in the television industry and he supposed I could give them ideas on Voronezh, the things I'd enjoyed seeing. We stopped at the foot of an apartment complex and SashaZ let out a loud cry that level-headed people don't do in public. A head popped out of a window on the second story and spoke in a more sensible tone. The figure met us around back and swiftly took us to the room upstairs. Maxim introduced himself as the coordinator and host of a TV show for ORT, the national network. Pointing to people, he introduced Abram the cameraman and Fedor the soundman. In the center of the room sat a tripod loaded high with a television camera. Maxim asked if I could be interviewed for a show. He said Russia would love a twenty minute spot on someone who had crossed half the globe to be there. What did he see? What did he like? What does he do? Why did he come? I obliged with an excitement I hoped didn't show.

Sitting down in a corner chair, I began an introduction as the camera fired to life. They asked a variety of questions and my answers were translated through SashaZ with me interrupting to emphasize the Russian words I knew. I tried to look happy, eager, and full of importance. Maxim cut the questions short and said we would move out to the Duma; the rest of the interview would take place at the foot of Lenin in Lenin's Square. I answered a few more questions there when Maxim

sighted Koltsovsky Park. The park sits across from the State
University and it was filled with students lunching or wasting
time until class. As we entered the park with the camera,
tripod, boom, and crew, I felt insecure. I was among my
students and scores of people who knew me by face. Maxim
directed me to do a confident walk in the thick of the
students. We did this many times before Maxim was satisfied.
They asked me if I was able to give them some time the
following day and I agreed to meet them for the finishing
segment.

The next afternoon I met the crew at the statue of Peter The
Great. There was a discussion about the day's content. I had
been asked about my feelings on the local culture and what I'd
seen. I truthfully had been amazed at the Kamerny Theatre, the
Opera, the ballet, and the philharmonic but these had been
personal and, with some regret, new to me. I hadn't attended
my share of the local arts scene at home. I did my best to
provide the setting in my mind, to express myself like a foreign
poet would. Maxim was happy regardless of what I gave him;
he only wanted me to be talking. This, I am sure, is because the
editing job will cut and paste me into the person he wanted
anyway.

'Good, good Brant. I wonder if you go to train station
tomorrow. Golden Mask award we did win. I want you to
present them. I want you to welcome them,' Maxim said. It was
funny but Maxim's fluency in English came and went.

'*Konyeshna*, of course,' I said.

Bright and early the following morning, I stopped by the
Institute and notified Marina that I may be the slightest bit late
for my first class.

'Ah mister television-star… forgive my stunted enthusiasm… who are you thinking will cover your class?' she asked.

'Well, I kind of figured I'd just let them all wander away,

heh-heh… get it? I'd just come and teach whoever remained behind.' I said it with the same tone she had asked.

'Russia doesn't need another comedian. We're trying to export them.'

'Marina, this is a big deal for me. I'm going to be on Russian television.'

'So?' she said.

'I was raised in Surrey,' I confided to her.

'What does that mean?'

'A lot…'

'I don't under-'

'Usually when people from Surrey are on that side of the camera,' I said, 'It isn't a good thing.'

'All right mister Brant, I'll make sure most of them are still here when you arrive.'

'*Spacebo*,' I said with a bit of a bow. I leant in for a kiss.

'*Obyu,*' she said invoking the friendly 'I kill you' phrase and she turned towards the window.

'Don't ever lose that light in your eyes,' I said as I stole her mouse ball.

I met up with Lucia. She had decided to come along after a few lonely hours pounding Italian into the keyboard. On the platform was a veritable parade. There were hundreds of people present for the Gala. There were banners and champagne, whistles and costumes. When I made my way through the crowd to Maxim and the crew, he told me that the Golden Mask Award was not unlike the Academy Awards in America. Suddenly I felt inadequate and anxious. This was now a major event and my face would be broadcast through living rooms and barbershops across the empire. Lucia drank champagne and tried to look good for Maxim. I considered taking a plate of champagne into a washroom stall and drinking my way to confidence but there was a loud, long, hollow horn. The train pulled in and the

actors could be seen looking out at their welcoming committee.
As they disembarked, Maxim briefed me on what to say. I
struggled for breath. Cameras started off right in front of my
face with their bright bulbs exposing every pore in my nervous
face. Where the hell was my translator? If I unleash my Russian
on them, I thought… but SashaZ squeezed through the crowd at
the last second.

'Thanks for coming comrade.'

'Sorry,' he said, 'Make-up sex.'

'I did *not* want to hear that.'

I traded hand shakes and introductions and told the actors
who I was. Maxim handed me a big, heavy box. I slid off the
ribbons and opened it and found five golden masks. I pinned
one on each of the actors' chests and received for it a crushing
hug. Cameras hovered.

Before we knew it, the platform was nearly empty and we
were left behind. The actors had gone off to do whatever they
needed to do after a twelve hour journey from Moscow, which
was probably drink. Maxim thanked me and said that I had to
attend the Kamerny Theatre that night. I was a guest of honour.
Although it was Milorad Pavich's *Forever and a Day* again, it
was a celebratory affair and all the heads of the city were to be
present. I agreed and since she was tugging at my sleeve, I
asked if Lucia could come. The seating in the Kamerny was
limited but Maxim jotted down a note on a pad of paper.

'Pick up ze tickets at booth okay, okay?' he said. 'Do not
forget Brant… you are ze man! Who is ze man?'

'Brant is ze man,' I said.

Marina was out when I went to ask her if I could hold my
classes in the park. Without her consent, I held my classes in
the park. The first class was with the third years and we
reviewed several pages of the textbook rather quickly but no
one's heart was keen on studying. Usually the Russians were

into studying anything with a voracious appetite. But here in the park, the novelty of English wore off quickly and soon the students were coming back from the kiosk with beer. I told them I was displeased, disappointed, and shocked not to mention jealous and nostalgic that they'd bought beer during class. I declined my next natural impulse and bought a flat Pepsi.

The second class was held at the park as well and when things got a little boring, I told them to go and get a beer. It was amazing the effect a little alcohol had on their participation. Perhaps my unorthodox teaching skills were just what the education system needed. Little Olga, who was shy and with-drawn, became a chatterbox. I was as surprised as the rest of the class. Karmen demonstrated fine English skills that no one knew she possessed. Kimi, a young woman with a stutter became a fluid piece of English machinery. She wouldn't, or possibly couldn't, stop. Others just sat with their faces in their hands awaiting a turn to speak. Perhaps the administration should consider this an unlikely boost for the national finals. It was, however, difficult to correct pronunciation when the subjects began slurring. The second year class ended in the late afternoon. I left the class at the foot of the steps leading into the Institute and waited for Lucia to come down.

The Kamerny Theatre was an outstandingly decorated venue that night. This was a special night for this small city. It was, for us, like looking in on the inner workings of a little world. The local news media was there, along with prominent Duma members. As soon as we approached, Maxim spotted me and drew me in front of the camera. The powerful lamp was turned on and the film began flowing. Maxim affixed a small microphone to my lapel. I was introduced to the theatre's resident director, the theatre's creator and the producer. I worked through SashaZ I lowered my lids and bowed my head conveying that this theatre was 'art' personified. Soon it was time for the presentation to begin. Lucia and I walked into the seating area. Maxim instructed, for reasons I shall never know, the cameraman to sit focused on me with his blazing light. Everyone in the room was looking at me. I would have looked at me too; I'd have asked who I was, what I was doing. For ten minutes, I was the center of attention and the subject of whispers. Lucia, seated beside me, began joking about how ridiculous it was to be making a scene as they were. She soon got angered and called Maxim a *slovnitski* (piss-ant little nothing) and quite soon after that, Maxim walked up to me from across the room and removed the lapel microphone. The camera went off as well. Lucia's head fell between her shoulders.

Maxim was a professional and appeared not to notice our embarrassment. He came and squatted in front of us and asked if we would meet the crew in the foyer for interviews during the intermission. Both Lucia and I enjoyed the first half of the show for our second time. We both, however, decided that we'd seen it enough. After I did two short intermission interviews, we snuck out the back door.

The building that houses the Kamerny Theatre is made up of a few different areas. We found ourselves in the alley listening to a second-storey class practice authentic Russian dancing. Lucia and I climbed on a small garage roof and peered in. There was a hardwood floor which had seen better days. Atop it were dancing, swinging, knee-slapping boys and girls. They were practicing hard and dripping with sweat. The male teacher spotted us and came to the window ready to punch. Lucia exercised her quick Russian skills and explained that we were both rather fond of the traditional Russian dance.

Gavril, the teacher, explained, 'Ha, it is paradoxical. We are the last traditional dance class in the city.' He splayed his hands across the room of young faces. 'How ironic it is that foreigners should say they love our work. We no longer get funding from the state.'

We looked in and saw that the only music they had was a very old man flexing his accordion. Gavril offered us to show up the following week, same time, to watch from inside the class. We told him we would and climbed down from the roof.

My birthday was a quiet affair. Anya wanted time alone with me and so it happened that no one else came to visit me on this day. Anya had baked a birthday cake. It was delicious, stacked high of pancakes and loaded full of strange, chewy nuts and hard raisins. I had Russian birthday cards and a small affordable gift. I had now spent birthdays in Canada, America, Estonia, Mongolia, and Russia. I remember thinking I was now 'old'. Thirty felt like a trophy for my 20s but thirty-one had felt like an unpaved highway to forty. I was older than Playboy center-folds. I wasn't ever going to be in the NHL, I would not be going into combat, and I would never luge competitively.

I spent a lot of time diligently trying to find the fastest way for a Russian to immigrate into Canada. Saddened with my results, Pavel went to war.

The school's president's son's chances at a life abroad would be determined by the *Test Of English as a Foreign Language* (TOEFL). This test is international and required by Canadian, British, American universities and other institutions of further learning. Having done the TOEFL instructor's preparation course, I was elected escort to Moscow and would be tearing apart our spoken language with Alyosha on the overnighter.

The TOEFL comprehension level requires strong conversational English. The Russian accent did, as of late, tend to give me migraines but Alyosha looked bound abroad. I would suffer through the areas he would be tested on. As a teacher, this was where I was needed.

This test was relatively expensive in Russian terms, costing the equivalent of three months wages for most people and was therefore like the golden ring from an inside horse on the merry-go-round of Russian life. TOEFL was beyond reach of nearly every student I taught. Financially that is, not linguistically. The TOEFL exam merely qualifies one for education abroad, it does not get you a job nor does it cover airfare overseas or the 11-hour train ride to take it. It is a mark.

And so it went at seven o'clock in the evening that I met Sasha and Alyosha on the platform. Sasha had somehow made his presence indispensable and managed to get the school to let him come. The honourable Mr. Zolotovinski and his wife were there as was Alyosha's younger brother Sergei. It was a crisp night and we waited among the various trains that were meeting the timetable. There is the 19:35 to Rostov; there comes the 19:50 from Sochi.

Our train eased onto the front rail and Alyosha hugged his family goodbye. A large woman with furry hands checked our tickets. The train jerked and we slowly began to move by the platform. As the Zolotovinskis drew behind us, so too did the stationhouse. Voronezh, in a hail of lights, fell away. Alyosha was keen to get to work on his English. He was not going to win any awards with his spoken English; he had never seemed too eager to learn anything on our walks and never bothered to clear up his critical problems. I had started out helping him at every mistake he made though he would carry on using the wrong tense, case or gender. I then elected to stay out of his learning when he repeated everything just as he had and became his friend, not his teacher. Here, under the thin light of the train's quarters, Sasha and I began to teach English from the ground up. When Alyosha began to tire, we all stretched back on the beds and slept. And while we slept, my segment on Voronezhian arts was aired on the country's television channel. Many people would watch it, many people would tell me I did an excellent job, but no one would think to tape it because you can't rent VCRs.

Moscow was under high cloud and boasting an above-average temperature. It took four subway trains to get Alyosha to his test. This was because Sasha was determined that he knew how to follow the small underground map we had purchased. In Moscow there are a variety of linkages in the subway system that cross one another but the most helpful are the 'ring road' trains which do entire circles of the city. It was rush-hour and the trains were packed to their limits. We had to backtrack at one point, one glorious moment where an 'I told you so' was warranted. I poked him hard in the chest.

We made it to Oktyabraskaya station and with minutes to spare, we entered the testing school. There were three students in the waiting hall with us, one of them practicing aloud. None of them spoke English anywhere near Alyosha's level. It was sad that they were spending so much hard earned money on the exam but likely weren't going to pass. I knew the test approach and thought Alyosha had a reasonable chance of passing.

An exam teacher approached, took his paperwork and signaled to Alyosha to follow. He entered a test room where there would be cameras at every corner to catch anyone cheating. I felt for the young Alyosha, both good and bad. His father's pressure had put a lot of stress on him.

Sasha and I left into the Moscow morning and spent the hours catching trains to places we didn't want to go. I had not signed in officially to the Canadian Embassy as is required if

one would like to expedite through any problems, injuries, or
deaths that arise, so we set our sights on getting across town.
After catching a number of trains, we made it to the Arbat
which was alive and full of tourists at the noon hour. Just off to
the side, across from the KFC and down a small road named
Starokonyushenny Pereulok, was the Canadian Embassy.
Draped from a rusty rod hung a Canadian flag. Sasha had
already reserved himself to standing outside while I conducted
my affairs.

'No,' I said, 'You can come and stand inside, on my home
and native land.'

'At the American Embassy, Russians must wait outside…
they do their business through a small window on the street,' he
said shyly.

I'd yet to enter the grounds but I was damned if my country
was going to let a friend stand out in the street. I encouraged
him on, finally taking his arm. We were warmly welcomed by a
French-Canadian man in a security uniform. He said 'Bienv-
enue-welcome' and showed us inside the waiting room. There
was no one else but us. I told Sasha a few French jokes and
fingered through the Canadian magazines.

I was called to the window as Sasha sat there, twiddling his
fingers uncomfortably. He felt like he was beyond his measure.
I went to the booth where two babushkas waited patiently. I
smiled and put forth my passport. I began to speak of my tardi-
ness and the hassle of the weather. The woman sitting down
held up her hand to stop me from going any further. They did
not speak English. I was stunned. I started speaking in French
but they did not speak that either. Right beside them, on the
window that shielded them from fits of rage, was a sticker that
said 'We speak English/French' but they only spoke Russian. I
didn't have the proficiency to convey all I wanted to say so I
turned in the chair and called to Sasha who was in mid-twiddle

of the Globe and Mail. I needed him to tell the ladies what I was there to do. He took small steps and seated himself on my side.

Through strange murmurings, we tackled the paperwork and filled it in. I was happily a registered ex-pat. I said thank you to the ladies in all three languages. I pressed them for some tokens of Canada to give out to my students, friends and co-workers. There was a short time in Canada where all you had to do to obtain a flag was make a phone call. But this pathetic experience ended with me being given two small Canadian pins. I had swept the entire Embassy clean of souvenirs.

Outside Sasha returned to his usual self. He had, he confided, felt very awkward inside. He stated that the way the American Embassy treated Russians was rather Russian but he never expected to be treated to the courtesy extended him in Canada's. I told him that we were like that and America was like that.

'Say Sasha, what would you say to lunch at the Duma?' I asked.

'The Duma? Do you really think we could have lunch at the Duma?' he said with excitement.

'The first rule of Canadian law,' I said, 'Is to never answer a question with a question.'

'Language laws?'

'You have no idea.'

'Then I will say yes, yes I would like to lunch at the Duma, I've never been. My Lord, who do you have connections with? Is it Putin? Because I like him. I just tell those jokes because-'

'It's okay Sasha… it's Zhirinovsky'

That shut him up for the whole hour it took to get there. On the steps of the Duma, I called Igor on a house phone. Since Igor's English was next to nothing, Sasha held the conversation in Russian. Igor exited and sharp handshakes were traded around. We passed through the security guards with their wands and went up to the tenth floor. Igor instructed us to sit, as I had before with Dad, in the large room dedicated to bad pictures of Vladimir Zhirinovsky. There was a very large cardboard cut-out of him with the words *Ja Znayou Kak Nado!* or 'I know what to do!'. It was an elaborate room that reinforced Zhirinovsky's skewed vision every time he passed through it. Sasha and I could see Zhirinovsky tipping back in a chair. He took no notice of us. But from the same room emerged Igor with a care package of Zhirinovsky memorabilia. There were Zhirinovsky video tapes, Zhirinovsky books and an LDPR t-shirt that I supposed would be best worn under another shirt.

The cafeteria was a great sight. I looked around wondering what information I had in my head that I could sell. Igor insisted that Zhirinovsky pick up the tab and I was in no financial position to argue since Zhirinovsky wasn't doing much to get me a regular paycheque. I had a beef item with a jolly dollop of potatoes. Sasha ordered a soup and some vegetable platter with dip. I couldn't tell what Igor had ordered but it had eyes and skin.

Sasha and I finished and left Igor in the lobby. There was a small mall of sorts and I purchased flower seeds for my grandfather (I discovered it was illegal to send them by mail the day after I'd sent them by mail). When we were done, we crossed the city to the TOEFL offices where Alyosha was finishing up.

Alyosha exited with a beaming face. He was confident he'd passed the test. I was proud of him and so was Sasha. We treated him to a gooey burger at a small chicken restaurant around the corner.

There was some time to wait before our train to Voronezh. We were only a short stroll from Gorky Park. Inside of the park, along the Moskva riverfront, sits *Buran*, the Soviet Union's space shuttle. After the Cold War, the mighty powers that be

retired it and they placed it at Gorky Park for all to see, speculate about, and admire. It was wasted on Sasha and Alyosha,
Buran was. This had been a major piece of the Space Race, the
mother of Mir. They didn't care to see it and they weren't even
prepared to spend the money on the entrance to the park, which
was nominal. I told them I'd be twenty minutes at most since
Buran was wedged fairly deep into the park. They would wait.

I made my way through a glorious spring evening, seemingly alone in the entire park. I could see Buran's massive tail
parting the trees. My heart was thumping. She was a gorgeous
piece of old technology. I fumbled through my pack and posi-
tioned my camera at her. I stood in different places and couldn't
get myself a decent picture of the craft. The damn fence was too
high, too thick and too black. I had a thought that I first
dismissed. Then I had it again. Could I squeeze through the
gate? I looked around and saw no one. The park was empty. I
moved to the padlock and fidgeted with it for one long second.

'What are you doing?' a voice behind me barked in Russian.

'ACK!' I yelled. What *was* I doing? Would he believe the
picture story? I began to piece together my Russian excuse. I
wanted a photo of Buran because... well, I was Canadian, I
loved space travel, I might write about Russia and well, I
wasn't American.

The thin man laughed and introduced himself as Grisha.
From the scent of his breath and his attempt at tying his shoe, I
could tell that he was drunk. Hmm. Grisha palmed a key ring.
He jabbed one into the padlock and swung the gate open wide.

I was unleashed into the burial ground for Buran. I took
shots of the nose, the wings and the landing gear. I was ecstatic
and burned through a roll of film. When I considered myself
done, Grisha, who had since taken to a lawn chair, threw his
head toward the staircase leading inside the beast. Did I want to
go inside Buran? Of course I did. But wait, drunken Russian

men don't offer anything for free, except hugs. Grisha offered a trip inside for one hundred rubles. I agreed. '*Xa-xa*,' said Grisha as he led me up the stairs.

The cockpit looked like it was from a 1950s space movie. It didn't look anywhere near advanced enough to launch itself into the stratosphere. It had far fewer buttons and gadgets than most commercial jet-liners, in fact most washing machines. I snapped pictures and followed Grisha into the payload dock. There was a theatre designed to show movies of the triumphs of Buran but since I was visiting on an off-day, I would not get to see the film. However just standing in Buran was enough. I had already given Grisha the hundred rubles but he insisted I sit down in a seat and wait for him. I sat alone in Buran for fifteen minutes. I knew that Sasha and Alyosha were anxious, if not mad, that I hadn't returned. When I could wait no longer, I exited Buran, and stepped down the stairs. Grisha was sitting in his lawn chair with a smile and an armload full of stuff. He looked like he was trying to figure out where he'd left me or why he was holding an armload full of stuff. He gave me a Buran poster, a Buran picture and something so incredible, I found it hard to contain myself. Sergei passed me a tile off Buran, one of the ceramic thermal protection re-entry tiles that faced two thousand degree heat. It was signed with a number and Russian characters. It came in its own little plastic case. I was agog and made a sophisticated noise like 'eeeeeee'. It was worth far more than the hundred rubles I told him. He looked as though I might pay him more. Instead I told him that I would write about him when I got back to Canada. So Grisha, 'here's to you'.

I had made us late. Dangerously late. The three of us began running and soon we were running at top speed. We crossed an eight-lane freeway and a muddy field. I spotted a Metro 'M' down a side-street and hollered to Sasha and Alyosha that we were nearly safe. As per the transit map, we were four trains from reaching Pavelyetskaya. We had 26 minutes. It began to rain. I wasn't so worried for myself, for if I didn't make the train, I could catch one the following day. But not returning the presidents' son on time would not be good for my employment record. We made each Metro connection like clockwork and approached Pavelyetskaya Station running at full speed. I saw it first; the entire station was roped off with police tape and emergency vehicles. We ran up to a police officer who told us that there was a bomb threat. He said the building was closed but that the trains were still leaving out the back. Hurriedly, we sprinted around the back, down the platform and left after 37 seconds on the train. Sasha and Alyosha looked like shit.

Once you are in Russia, especially into the birch forests and villages, you can *feel* the border wrapped around you like an electrified fence. Since Russia is still striving to be a threat, spying is alive and well and no foreigner is exempt from being an attractive curio. In the streets people can smell that you don't fit. A cane-dependant old man once demanded proof that I was Canadian. In the middle of the street, with the #43 tram approaching, I flipped my passport and unmistakable two-dimensional self at him. The last foreigner many people in small-town Russia saw was German. That year was 1945. For me to blend in, particularly with a collar-up trench coat and fedora, seemed remote.

What troubles Russians most is just what an outsider can understand *of* them. Surely you must *be* Russian in order to understand her, they exude. You can't earn or be granted a citizenship. You need the genes, particularly that noisy one at the end that the other genes don't talk to anymore. Russia is sacrosanct and so anyone who forfeits a high GDP to live in Russia is obviously dabbling in espionage. The very word *espionage* conjures up laser crosshairs, shrines of microfilm secrecy and concerned unibrows. When you leave work intent on eating a bag of Kuprinikalinjimskis and crashing on the couch, your peers will see you slicing through the crowds on your way to a black and white courier box. If you leave at lunch to see one girlfriend rather than deal with the estrogen collision of seeing her after work which is when another is coming by, then the office will be convinced you have transferred the school's floor plans to a spy for another school. I hadn't seriously thought I'd be directly confronted with spying. I was not persuasive enough to remove all doubt. At this time, there was an American student charged with possession of a small quantity of marijuana and the authorities accused him of spying. He was a student at the State University where I taught English. We never met. In all my travels, the one thing I resent is the American over-presence in other countries and I refrain from meeting any Americans I can in foreign lands. These days you can't sneak into the jungle and meet jungle-people without them telling you in pictographs that you resemble Jack Simpson Jr., the man who left his flag, Bible, and McNugget sauce. But the student's arrest and subsequent trial left me explaining myself.

Spies were being caught in Russia and the United States alike. Diplomats were being expelled tit-for-tat. On the other hand, I couldn't spy effectively for reasons of luck. I nearly lost my guardian angel in a mafia confrontation years ago and we haven't seen eye to eye since. I've been accidentally electrocuted more than the common person. From plane crashes to psychotic hitchhikers to tow truck accidents to carbon monoxide nights and Autobahn accidents, I've survived kicking luck in the nuts a few times. But if I tried to spy, I would be caught a month before I decided to do it.

The end of the school year was approaching; the end of my teaching assignment loomed. Lucia and I talked about the final days. I considered the possibility of her and I going to Kazakhstan or Mongolia. I said I would earn just enough to keep us both there for a few months. I was teasing her, with promises that couldn't yet be made. I had tried for but hadn't secured a position in either country and if it paid anywhere in the neighbourhood that Russia was paying, it wouldn't be enough for two people. I didn't want to think of leaving Lucia; she gave me perspective. She taught me what Russia was to a foreigner. Without her, there were no ropes and pulleys. She was my Rosetta Stone. It's funny how sometimes you can meet a person and wonder how you ever lived without them because of what they add to your experience. The teachers and the students would stay with me forever but they were meant to leave. They were supposed to be memories, the specific memories one hopes to have, to hold and to carry with you in life. But Lucia was like a guidebook, sometimes an irritating one that often flew unprovoked into a crazy Italian fit, but a guidebook nonetheless. Our nights listening to Italian opera spanned three seasons yet seemed to me as only a night or two.

And I could see in Anya's eyes that she knew I was going to be leaving her soon. I had only recently told her to return to her psycho-relatives. It seemed to surprise her that the time she was allowed to stay still ended with her moving out. It was like taking the breeze from a bird in flight. Through the tears and choking fits of sadness, she gradually accepted the arrangements. After her suicide plots and many nights calming her down, I realized that she was more than I could handle.

'I wanted to be your once in a lifetime', she whispered.

'You are…' I said back.

Alyosha failed his TOEFL exam.

.   .   .

I had six rolls of undeveloped film. I hadn't thought to take them to the shop until I took my last picture of a fire truck racing down Koltsovskaya. I grabbed the rolls, walked to the Konica store and dropped them off. I returned in three hours and the familiar Konica lady handed out six packages of photographs.

With the packages in hand I headed the short stroll back home. There were several babushkas on the bench, taking advantage of the drying sky and cursing their husbands. Six men were playing a game of cards at the other end of the table. All of them I recognized; all of them recognized me. I thought it would be original if I showed some pictures since photographs were fairly expensive. I generously handed out my pictures with explanations that seemed to be understood. Someone else arrived with a bottle of vodka and sat down.

'*Krasavista*,' the babushkas remarked, beautiful. Others made them pause and ask why I photographed such things. There were broken grates, sickles, ten men trying to fix a broken down car, dogs. A few I had to hide from them, a few weren't meant for anyone else to see.

Suddenly, from the corner, rounded two militsia. They stepped sharply. I had never seen them near the back of my building. And these two men were there for a purpose. They grabbed my pictures, shoved them back in the packages, twisted my arms together and handcuffed me. Then they dragged me away.

'Clearly this is a mistake,' I said nervously in parts of three languages.

I caught sight of the old babushkas with their mouths agape. I heard them whispering as I was hauled away. I had no idea what was happening and the militsia didn't say a word. I was led across the street to a small holding cell near the kiosks. I was thrown into the wooden structure, no larger than an outhouse. I stood there watching groups of roving militsia come by and flip through my pictures. Perhaps they'd never seen someone develop six rolls of pictures. Neither Lucia nor I had ever developed more than one roll at a time.

In the back of my head were a few thoughts: first, photographing anything in the Soviet Union was a risky venture. Secondly, it might not be as *glasnost* as I thought. Maybe I'd just been ambling back with over a hundred pictures of guilt in my hands. Could the people who developed the film have called? Did they see something I shouldn't have photographed? It wasn't long ago that pictures taken by foreigners in Russia were censored. Now here I was, in a tiny jail cell and six police officers were going through my printed memories.

I waited.

Hours on, as the sun was setting, I slumped down and slept.

When I awoke, it was with four strong hands grabbing my shoulders. It was dark. They pulled me along and threw me into the back of a paddy wagon-type vehicle. I was terrified. Suddenly everything was a whole other level of serious. I'd read about Moscow's Lyubyanka prison and feared we'd reach there by morning. But we travelled only ten minutes, during which time the driver cornered sharply enough several times to throw me about the darkness. We came to an abrupt stop. The doors were flung open and I was yanked out by my jacket collar. The first thing and the last thing I saw was a flight of concrete stairs. Before I could brace myself, I was thrown down them. I hit my head and fell unconscious.

I came to and realized that things were very bad. I was in a cell with five other men. I couldn't walk, couldn't even stand. My legs were numb from the knees down and everything north of that hurt. I'd been stripped and left in my underwear. The room was dark except for three small toaster-size windows that reflected faint light from a distant streetlamp. I struggled to raise myself but was pushed down by the gang of men in the room. They were jabbering in Russian about the new arrival. My head was swollen, throbbing. And my elbows and knees were bleeding. I could feel the warm liquid all over my hands. My ribs felt broken, aching at my short breaths. I tried to make it to a cot and was kicked off it by one of the goons. I pulled myself onto another and someone flipped it upside down on me. I tried feebly to explain that I was Canadian.

'Ja Canadiets,' I said offering dialogue. They responded with slang I didn't understand. Someone grabbed one of my legs and dragged me around. One of the men picked me up and held me by my neck with both hands until my feet were off the floor. He yelled a Russian phrase that got laughs from the others. He let go, and I crumpled to the ground. I stayed as quiet and motionless as I could.

The door swung open. Two guards came in and dragged me to a counter. I could barely limp. I was scared that I was now paralyzed for life. I couldn't stand at the desk, so I clung to it.

The main guard stood in front of me and two floated behind him, looking on. I was asked in Russian many questions about myself.

'*Emya*,' he said matter-of-factly, name.

'Brant,' I said.

'*Familya*,' he said without blinking, last name.

'Antonson.'

He had my passport beside him. 'Canadiets?'

Those were the formalities. Now how did a Canadian end up in front of him? I said I was a teacher, I gave him my address, I told him who I worked for. I asked why I was there. He replied in Russian that I had been drinking in public. I carefully thought out my response: No one was drinking at the time, and the vodka wasn't mine. The last time I had vodka, my flat became Area 51. Russians drink anywhere they want in public and even if the aforementioned was all ridiculously false, why was I the only one at that table who was lynched in a dark cell? But my Russian couldn't communicate these issues and I instead replied 'Nyet.' He had my packages of photos and one by one he carefully went through them. A few could be classified as 'art' in my definition. There were others, were I given the choice, I would not have elected for him to see; things that could be construed as un-touristy in the wrong light. And this was the wrong light. The guard slapped them on the counter. The Duma, Zhirinovsky's office, the Duma's limousine, a Chechnyan guitar player on the Arbat, Sheremetyevo's airfield, Sheremetyevo's Antonovs, and Sheremetyevo's luggage carousels. Vagrants, beggars, the department store, the market. Not to mention Anya wearing my Principessa tie and nothing else. Patiently, but emphatically he would flip a picture to me and ask its particulars. I tried with all my will to look innocent and feign knowledge. I was scared shitless. I was badly wounded. I needed a cigarette.

'*Mozhna… cigaryet?*' I asked.

The guard declined. I then asked for a cigarette each time he asked me about a picture. By the thirtieth time I was granted one cigarette and one match. It is odd how the simplest things in life can make a moment better. It may have been the best cigarette of my life because for the moment the circumstances were improved.

'*Spaceba bolshoy…*' I whispered.

When it burned to the filter, I was slammed into another cell with a different group of men. They thought I was a spy, the American jailed in Voronezh. I tried to make them aware that I was a Canadian teacher but they kept calling me the American's name. They pushed me to the walls and pummeled me with punches and kicks. There was no laughing, they really believed they were in the presence of a threat to their country. I sagged to the floor. I tried to grip onto a cot as I neared passing out. I felt fresh hands grip my throat and I was lifted up again.

'*Oochityel... angliski yazik*,' I said yet again, teacher... English language.

They finally gave up, dropped me to the floor and left me to deteriorate in the corner. I was stripped of all spirituality, all reason, all understanding.

I waited to die.

I stayed in the least painful position until dawn. New guards came and dragged me out. I sensed that I was going to be released. I was led to a cold, bare room to wash off the blood and get dressed. My nice clothes, trench coat and fedora were in a pile. I found all my money and my negatives gone. My passport and most of my pictures were stacked in a pile.

A guard prodded me to move faster. He pointed to a door and left. I made it to the door and found myself in a bright day, at the bottom of the stairs I'd been thrown down.

Walking consisted of locking my knees with both hands. I made it up the stairs and slowly crossed the dusty precinct lot, pain balancing pain. I had no idea where I was. I flagged down a car and tried to explain that all my money was at home. The driver looked me up and down and drove off. A fourth car pulled over, the driver took pity, and drove me home.

Back at my apartment, Anya was devastated. She'd spent the night wide-awake wondering where I was and imagining the worst had happened. I told her it had. Anya called the school and notified Marina that I'd been in jail. Within twenty minutes Marina was in the apartment and making calls to her mother. At some point it must have crossed Marina's mind to say 'why is a student here Brant?' But she didn't. Undoubtedly a whole lot of stuff was suddenly suspicious to her. To everyone.

I was taken to a hospital for medical check-ups. No one ever wants to be in a hospital and no one ever really, really, really, really wants to be in a Russian hospital. Three ribs were cracked. I had a concussion. The diagnosis for my legs was inconclusive and from that moment on, I was going home for treatment. Home to Canada. I was shattered. I was horribly depressed and wounded. I sent home frantic emails about being beaten in a Russian jail. I should have put more thought, care, and attention into those emails because they sparked a horrible anxiety in the people I cared for.

I convalesced in my room, Anya taking care of every need. I was in perpetual shock. I was going home for sure. There would be no Kazakh steppes or Mongol retreats, there was only an urgent ride to the country where they could best treat me. I was reluctant to follow my family's wishes but I knew that I could not run and hide, especially not run.

When Petrovich, head of security for the school, went down to the police station to see what I had been hauled in for and what had happened to me while in the militsia's custody, there were no files on me. There was no record of my night from hell. There was nothing saying I had ever been there and no one remembered me.

Sasha had phoned my father and in his version of English recounted what had happened. This was not helpful. When I had time alone, I phoned my Dad.

'What happened?'

'I don't know... but this has Russia written all over it.'

'How are you doing?'

'I think Russia went Soviet on me last night.'

'Oh no.'

'Can you wire me $5000?'

'WHAT?'

'I need some time to think... that would help,' I said.

'No, you are coming home. At least you are up top, not cargo.'

'Does anyone at the U.N. owe you a favour?'

'Did nurses medicate you again?'

'I'm working on some strategies.'

'Forget it. Brant is coming home.'

'But I'll just be *Brent* there...'

'Son, I know this is a difficult ending to a great time in Russia. You've made incredible strides as an individual... you've gotten through a hard year of teaching in a country that you love. You've had amazing friends and girlfriends and made memories of things many people can't picture. Come home, get well... write about it.'

'Home...' I said, 'Is just so… *home'*.

'Come back to Vancouver, get better, write, and teach again. Of course you may prefer a different country. Like Switzerland... Iceland.'

Dad told me that Sean and Hilary had been unceremoniously rerouted from Ireland and directed towards Voronezh on a rescue mission. There was a mess of paperwork to be done in order for them to get in to Russia quickly. Sasha did all he could, pulling Russian strings. In the days leading up their arrival, I moved around a bit. Dependant on Anya's shoulder, I made my way out to the kiosks. I hobbled over tram tracks and idled down Koltsovskaya. I felt deathly unwell. Through my pain and stuttering gait I appreciated my beloved city for the last times. I would not be able to mount the staircases required to teach, and therefore I did not teach. As those were the final weeks of school, it was not surprising to all that I was leaving but to those who saw me, hobbling about, I was an unpleasant sight.

I couldn't see much out my window for the display of leaves and it felt isolating and claustrophobic. Lucia spent a lot of time with me and for some reason she kept talking about the leaves. Life was filled with discontentment. Since the police incident, everything had a different angle to it. Maybe I had a different angle to me. I never asked. I just noted in my long days that there was a compassion towards me that I didn't want. There was an unsaid ghost of me already lingering about. Lucia seemed close but in such a way as though I had already left her. Our nightmares of a bad ending to Russia had come true.

This could have become an *international* news incident. Not the kind where prime ministers call presidents from red phones but it warranted being news in Canada. I did not take that step. I emailed very few people. I mean if I had stolen a mafia BMW and ran over a posse of babushkas, the media work would have been done for me. But this went silently beneath the radar of everyone but family and close friends. Without any paperwork or adequate proof except my own word, I did not alert my travel insurance company. I was still shaking my head at the way it all played out and had little authority on the matter in the big picture. It seems Russia had just reverted back to its past for one night, not content to let me leave without a brief glimpse of her unspoken reality.

Sean and Hil's train arrived in Voronezh a week after my encounter with the militsia.

'So you finally faced your fear of being beaten in a Russian jail,' Sean said. 'That's the first step.'

'It's great to see you, you've put on weight.'

'I'm supposed to be sipping Irish lagers in Belfast. It was the last country in Europe for us… plans to party it up for days. But noooo.'

'Yeah about that,' I said responsibly, 'Thanks for coming. It means a lot. Why don't we all go to Ireland?'

'You are going home. We'll stay at Sue's outside of London for a few days and then I am watching you get onto a plane. And I will see that plane take off.'

'Who is Sue?' I asked.

'She's a friend. She will drive you to said plane.'

'We'll talk about it.' I said.

'Something tells me there's going to be a lot of paperwork when you die.'

For two days, Sean and Hilary spent their time walking the city with Anya and Lucia as guides. Confined to my flat to start cleaning up, I packed my belongings and wondered at the amazing sequence of events in my life. Events of this caliber seem to happen to me periodically so, with Bach cello concertos on low, I made peace with the three dominant gods one afternoon (in hindsight, it didn't work.). My rooms already felt distant. I was grateful to see my brother but I had wanted to meet him in Istanbul, Sarajevo, Prague, even boring Belarus. It was nice for him to see my city, which he was sure he wouldn't get to visit, but the circumstances were all wrong. This 'rush' to get me home was too much for me; it was stealing my new life away. I spoke at length with my father and tallied up hundreds of dollars in charges. I told him I had become content to let the Russian doctors assess me and, if I was wounded for life, I didn't want to be wounded in Canada. I'd rather stagger out my remaining time in any other place on earth. Dad tried a variety of tactics to persuade me that it was best for me, that 'our' doctors and health care system were unparalleled, that certainly better medical services could be provided there instead of Russia. I didn't buy it. Instead I threatened to make my way to somewhere on the Siberian steppe with Anya as my fiancé and nurse. I'd become a shut-in counter-revolutionary fighting for the rights of shut-in counter-revolutionaries. Dad didn't buy it. And when I handed the phone to Sean, I knew Dad was making sure I didn't hobble out the door to Nor'ilsk.

I invested the physical effort and made it to the Institute for a meeting with the president. Sean and Hilary came to meet the man who had brought me to Russia. There was passive shock in his voice. He tried to thank me for all the work I'd done but I could tell he was still speechless over the actions of his country's police force. Maybe he wanted to say that developing six rolls of film all at once was pure stupidity. Perhaps he thought that the absence of any proof I'd been in jail was a cover-up for something I'd brought on myself.

I did my rounds and interrupted my students in classes. The struggle to walk to the front of the rooms was distressing. I stood before them with my hands clasped and mincing words about the great times we'd shared. I had bonded with my students. I was a friend, a confidant; I knew more about many of them than their own parents did. The crushing looks I received as I told them I was leaving drew tears to my eyes. My year was essentially over anyway; they had federal exams to take that I was not going to be a part of even if I did stay. But we'd never talked about me going home. Leaving is something that goes easier when you can share the times, relive the memories and look fondly back on the trials, many classes and the successes. Leaving because you have endured what I called 'an unnecessary use of Boris' is something that makes everyone involved look forlorn and distant. I mean, no one ever wants to be in jail and no one ever really, really, really, really ever wants to be in a Russian jail.

Slava cornered me and thanked me for being the part of his life I had come to be. He gave me a Somerset Maugham book and I gave it back to him. I handed him my copy of Bill Bryson's *In A Sunburned Country*. My suitcases were bursting as it was. We had shared a lot of great discussions. Nona, Olya and Nina bravely smiled and gave me pictures of themselves and notes to be read only when I'd left the tarmac. Tatyana, who was always running off somewhere, caught her breath and thanked me for taking care of her students, accenting that I had had an impact on their skills. Then she scurried off.

I called Natasha and broke the news to her. I sensed the wheels in her mind spinning with solutions. Maybe she could have someone shot for me. When Natasha insisted she come and visit me, I told her truthfully that it was better that she remember me the way I was and not as I was now. I said that's what I was trying to do. I explained to her that she meant a great deal to my soul, that she'd shown me a side of this city that would have otherwise gone unnoticed. Every moment had been electrifying. I said to keep it that way.

Igor spent a lot of time with me in the last week, hanging out with Sean and using the internet. I would miss him. Igor was a brother to me. We'd exchanged about 20 pounds of mementos over the time. I was leaving with gauges from the flight deck of a Tupulov, a tin cigarette holder, a brass pepper mill, and most of his juvenile Russian schoolbooks. I had gotten my old laptop back from Sasha and when I found myself with two computers, I told Igor that if he could come up with $50, I would give him the old one. While he made phone calls from my flat, Anya snuggled up to me. Despite the conflicts we had, she would be the hardest to leave. What would she do with her future now that we'd been so close? Where would she spend her time? Doing what? She said that she didn't feel like staying in Voronezh without me. She decided that it would be best if she moved to Estonia where her cousins lived. But Anya didn't have the money. The trip would cost her a minimum of $50. Igor returned from his sister-in-law's with a $50 bill that he'd no doubt double-crossed the devil to get and I handed him the laptop that we'd spent so many nights on, drinking chai, listening to Russian hip-hop and smoking cigarettes. He beamed. I rolled over and gave the money to Anya, convinced everyone was now better off with my departure. Anya welled up. I kissed the bridge of her nose and said something in Russian that neither of us understood.

Hours before Sean, Hilary, and I left town, I looked around my flat at the faces in my life. While it was amusing to see everyone talking, laughing, and using the last of my honey in their tea, the empty walls of the flat and the line-up of luggage spoke volumes. Marina showed up and dropped the information that the apartment was already leased out to a company in town. Marina and I talked, and then there was a strange pause between us. We just looked at each other with nothing to say. I shrugged my shoulders. She frumpled her lips and pouted. It was one too many goodbyes.

It came time to head for the station. Sean and Hil and Marina and Lucia and Sasha headed off in the school's Volga with the luggage. I took the tram with Anya. The cold seats, the sharp air, the muddy floor, the quivering wheels…Anya sat on my lap and silently pondered her future. I watched the city pull by in the last of the daylight. We arrived at the station and made our way to the train.

Slava had shown up and was ogling at Igor who stood happily cradling the laptop. It was a rare possession and I knew Slava was stunned that Igor had it. But enough of the politics, enough gossip and rumours. God knows what had been said at my schools about my departure. I could only guess that the truth had been embellished to the point where I was either being deported for spying, moving to a lavish suburb of Moscow, or heading home with a plethora of lethal Russian-borne diseases because I hadn't boiled the water. I'd only told a few people the truth.

All I did was mount the stairs, turn and wave. Sean and Hil

were fighting with the luggage as I looked stoically back at the Voronezh platform and all of my friends. As the train's providnitsa told me in Russian that I'd better not fuck with her on the trip, she pulled up the stairs and shut the metal door. What I had wondered about Voronezh with all my heart a short year before, was answered, terminated, and left behind. As the train moved to speed and I turned to head down the corridor, I caught sight of Anya pacing the train, crying and blowing kisses.

A CANADIAN SUMMER

.

After spending a week hobbling around England, I headed to Vancouver. There were thoughts that needed to be filed and injuries to contemplate. I bore the brunt of the long flight home. I didn't want to be home, I *needed* to continue my life somewhere else. I resented Vancouver, its excesses and its attributes. I had become a different person, a parallel self. Being at home felt like failure. I learned that my secure union job in Canada had vaporized. There were obvious concerns from friends and family and I did my best to appear well and healthy. My right leg became functional early on but for the next few months my left leg had no sensation, I couldn't command it properly and I was left with an annoying stumble. A specialist did nerve tests, neurological tests, and hit my kneecap with a little hammer a lot. The problem didn't show up in any results. After my car caught fire, I was forced to walk to the places I was used to driving to. That seemed to help the healing. I regained full use of my foot and learned to walk normally again. With my health bouncing back from the depths of a handicap, I turned my attention to constructing a new life, content that the 'me' in Voronezh and the 'me' I had left home to avoid in the first place, were memories. In their place was a new man, an unemployed new man without a car, who was prepared to face a new world.

A time came, months on, when I was losing my Russian mindset. I was, in the same breath, Russian and Canadian. I was in a mental superposition, a place where one life was seeping out and another was rushing in. I was becoming a New Canadian. I had broadband, a cell phone, good coffee, and taxes. I had back my Vancouver mountains, my Pacific Ocean, and my fertile farm-embossed Fraser Valley. I had paved roads, enormous bridges, skyscrapers, and traffic helicopters. There were teams of pedestrians out at lunch to get vegan-to-go or Starbucks lattes or 99 cent pizza slices. People drove to Costco on the weekend, rented movies, shopped in massive malls, bought legitimate CDs, took elevators, skied after work, kayaked at dawn, and developed several rolls of film. And not every SUV or BMW was suspect. I had recently been in a life where there was none of that. And yet I had still felt rich in Voronezh with what little there had been.

This is the lesson travel taught me. It is the result of contrast, the experience of differences and the essence of recognizing acute change. From being fluent in a new currency to managing oneself daily on a foreign public transit system, being adaptable and aware that you have adjusted to a whole new set of rules, turns life into a rewarding journey. Over time I would go through my pictures, read my notes and scrutinize my keepsakes. The positive memories of Russia became staples of my attitude, examples of personal achievement, and vitamins of confidence. But it wasn't easy to construct a manuscript about my time in Russia without feeling each and every moment of drama, knowing full well how it was going to turn out. Visiting aliens and jail beatings aren't easily assembled into text. One's own love and shame, confidence and sorrow, successes and failures, don't easily write their way into readable vignettes when it is written in first-person. The manuscript would be Brant's signature.

Russia is a formidable country, a land that defies a single description. It is so vast and varied that someone with an extensive teaching or travelling experience anywhere else in the same land may well gain exact opposite views on the people, features, and culture. I've no doubt some Russians will take offence at my conclusions. But Russia, diverse and immense, is filled with so many pockets of distinction that no one, Russian or foreigner, can rule out any personal experience. The population of Voronezh showed me how they fit in to the Russian landscape. Such glimpses became knowledge. Through my seasons there, this knowledge crafted a travelogue locked into an important time in the life of their country, it became a story…*of Russia.*

AFTERWORD

It's no surprise to anyone now that Russia invaded its neighbor, Ukraine, in February 2022. I have strong feelings about this. My friends in Russia have deeper convictions. But this book was devoid of the future possibilities of war, even when Russia took away Ukraine's Crimea region overnight in 2014 (just months after hosting the Olympic Winter Games in Sochi). Ukraine stood poised to be taken piece by piece if need be. The West had to step in.

This book covers a span of time closer to the collapse of the Soviet Union and further from territorial expansionism than anyone, but Putin could have predicted. As this war has unfolded for me, I can't help but think how stupid starting a ground war is. I used to say there were three keys to a successful life. One, find something you love to do. Two, find someone to do it with. And three, never attack Russia in the winter! Oh, that got a lot of laughs before the invasion. But the joke is on me.

If I was going to attack Ukraine (reminding myself I was once a Superpower), I would have detonated the Tsar-Bomba (the single most massive conventional bomb ever made) in

Independence Square in Kyiv, stopping the economy, stopping the electricity, and stopping the webcams. And then I would scare the entire country that war would soon be everywhere and escape was futile. But on the Maiden Square website, Kyiv 2024 looks as bustling as Kyiv 2020. The worst part about this war is how senseless it is. Chechnya was a different paradigm, another sort of war. But a ground war in Ukraine is just a machine to kill young men.

The Soviet Union was dismantled by three powers in 1990; Russia, Ukraine, and Belarus. The Commonwealth of Independent States (CIS) grew out of that, headquartered in Minsk, Belarus. These three countries are pivotal in organizing 12 member countries and ex-Soviet states. But we do remember that the Cold War, the Iron Curtain, and Soviet Communism fell together at the same time. Capitalism, freedom, and democracy won at the very same moment. This event held the potential for world peace if you can believe it. Such were the possibilities. But the timeline of being post-Soviet comrades seems to have only lasted a few meek decades, and now the West is again at war with Russia. Ironically we all pray to the god of the national gross domestic product; we hail the GDP.

It's also essential for me to let you know that the book you are reading caught a transition between past and future, Soviet and "essentially" free, with many examples of both lifestyles coexisting. It was because I experienced Russian culture, breathed the air, ate the foot, and loved the people that I could go and see places that would have been off-limits, sheltered, or prohibited, as some form of martial law covers Mother Russia.

And it is, therefore, within these pages, one may get the last sense of place for a Soviet life lived through 2000-2001. I also used the first digital camera in the city (and dropped it into five pieces). I had no cellphone as prices were reaching $500 for a phone. But I did have the only laptop at home in a city of a million people. There were only twenty computers available for the public to use. These were extraordinary times when Russians were grappling with the rapidly approaching future.

Such were the times when I would resign myself to writing, dating a girlfriend, and then writing some more. I wanted to convey to the world I was seeing and hearing these things first-hand to pass on to a world that Russia mystified. My backstory will clear up many questions about the transition from 1991 to 2014.

I hope the text stands as a breakwater for what transpires afterward. Russians do not deserve to be stuck behind another Iron Curtain – a variant of freedom has been the law of the land for thirty years. Again, I captured this dichotomy and exploited it for the reader. The book aimed to capture Russia in transition – before money moved in and built towers, ripped up the tram tracks, and swept away all the kiosks. Eight years after living there, I could hardly find my way around. I stopped caring what had been where. The Russia I had captured in a book simply no longer existed. Like a photographer capturing a spectacular event, I wrote it out instead. I had a snapshot of Russia that was 78,000 words long.

Indeed it was taking photographs that would lead to my demise. The Russian mindset - a unique psychological phenomenon - has a strong grip on the West, bringing them Levis, Xboxs, and McDonald's. For 70 years, they wondered about us as we wondered about them. The questions have been answered. The soul of Russia now has America written into it. Since there is no going back, what does the future hold?

B Antonson
    Anacortes,
    Washington State USA

Acknowledgments

I wish to thank the Russians in Voronezh who became a part of my life and let me be a part of theirs. For the sake of protecting their identities, while they are the characters in this story, their names have been changed. On 'Of Russia' as a manuscript, I am indebted to Rick Antonson, Marina Nestrugina, Jill Simpson, Brian Antonson, Robert Judge, Gordon Stewart, Asante Penny, Jeremy Antonson, Dianne Lyons, and Chris Bright. If there are assumptions or oversights, they rest with the author.

ABOUT THE AUTHOR

As a teacher and globetrotter, Brent Antonson spent years living abroad. His "other homes" have included Russia, Iraq, and China, where he taught English at universities and schools.

Of Russia; A Year Inside was first published in 2008, and more recently revamped and enhanced with his drawings for a new edition's release in 2024. This follows the 2023 publishing of *Ties That Bind: Circumnavigating the Northern Hemisphere by Train,* his second book. A prolific essayist, Brent's writing appears regularly on planksip.org and SubStack. He's written lyrics to several songs that have been recorded and released. One of his movie scripts awaits production. As an avid motorist, he has enjoyed driving escapades in all 50 American states, resulting in his first draft manuscript decades ago which remains safely tucked away in a storage locker. Though "being elsewhere" always figures in his future, Brent is tethered to the region of Vancouver, Canada (49.15'N 123.6'W) where he was raised.

Ties that Bind: Circumnavigating the Northern

Hemisphere by Train

"Antonson continues Paul Theroux's
tradition, but with a comic twist."
— Michael McCarthy, author of
*The Snow Leopard Returns: Tracking Peter Matthiessen
to Crystal Mountain and Beyond*

TIES THAT BIND

Circumnavigating the Northern
Hemisphere by Train

Brent Antonson

Author of *Of Russia: A Year Inside*

МИНИСТЕРСТВО ОБРАЗОВАНИЯ РОССИЙСКОЙ ФЕДЕРАЦИИ
ВОРОНЕЖСКИЙ ГОСУДАРСТВЕННЫЙ УНИВЕРСИТЕТ

No _179_

«22» _мая_ 200_1_ г.

394693, Россия, Воронеж, Университетская пл., 1.
E-mail: office@main.vsu.ru; INTERNET: www.vsu.ru
Телефон: (0732)789-420, (0732)789-674
Факс: (0732)789-755; (0732)552-836

English Philology Department
Romance and Germanic Philology
Voronezh State University
Universitetskaya pl., 1
Voronezh 394693
Russia
tel. ++(0732) 789489
fax ++(0732) 789388

21 June 2001

To whom it may concern

We have worked with Mr Antonson since November 2000, and soon came to know him as a very professional and well-organised colleague. During this time, he taught English to the second, fifth and sixth-year students of English Philology.

Whilst working at Voronezh University, Mr Antonson displayed excellent professional skills and initiative. He is diligent, responsible and hardworking. He is able to communicate with people at all levels and feels comfortable either in a leadership position or as a team-worker. He has coped extremely well with his work at the university during a difficult transitional period in Russia, proving himself to be very flexible and adaptable to new situations and having an excellent ability to solve unexpected problems. Mr Antonson has demonstrated qualities which could also be applied to a business environment and we would highly recommend him to any future employer.

Dr Natalya Sharova
Head of the English Philology
Department

Dr Lubov Tsurikova
Reader
English Philology Department

МИНИСТЕРСТВО ОБРАЗОВАНИЯ
РОССИЙСКОЙ ФЕДЕРАЦИИ

МУНИЦИПАЛЬНОЕ
ОБРАЗОВАТЕЛЬНОЕ УЧРЕЖДЕНИЕ

ВОРОНЕЖСКИЙ
ЭКОНОМИКО-ПРАВОВОЙ
ИНСТИТУТ

Россия, 394036, Воронеж, ул. Кольцовская, 23/1
Телефон: (0732) 727-375, Т/факс (0732) 727-371
E-mail: mail@vilec.ru
ОКПО 49732361

To Whom It May Concern

I write this in support of the application of Mr. Brent Antonson for a position in your organization. I first met Mr. Antonson in November 2000 in Voronezh, Russia where he was teaching English at Voronezh Institute of Law & Economics (VILEC). Since that time and up to June 2001 I worked in constant and close contact with him.

During his work at VILEC Mr. Antonson has shown himself as a resourceful and effective instructor who is responsive to the individual learning needs of his students and is able to help them develop to their full potential. Moreover, he is well versed in in the economic, political, social, and educational problems of Canada, Russia and other foreign countries he visited. His knowledge of a number of multi-cultural environments is considerable and immediate. His extensive expertise in cross-cultural communications allows him to be a valuable bridge between Canada and Russia, and other countries in order to foster communications and understanding between the nations in the global world.

Having been in constant contact with Mr. Brent Antonson over the last eight months, I have had an opportunity to know him from different perspectives. He has considerable expertise and excellent practical skills in information technology, especially in working in the Internet environment. Mr. Antonson has distinguished himself by his and professional approach to travelling and living in multi-cultural environments. His international experiences are not just "pleasure" and "entertainment" for him, but he feels interested and committed to learn and get insight into life of other countries and peoples. As a result of his trips to Russia he has written a book on Russia which, due to its insights, sophisticated observations and lively style may present considerable interest for experts and general public both in Canada and in other countries.

Mr. Brent Antonson is a man of integrity, has effective communication skills, he is a friendly, open person, and a good team worker. I strongly recommend Mr. Brent Antonson for a position in your organization.

For further information or verification please contact

Dr. Valery Makoukha, Vice President for International Programs, Voronezh Institute of Law & Economics
Tel.: (0732) 71-68-66 E-mail: val@vilec.ru

www.ingramcontent.com/pod-product-compliance
Lightning Source LLC
Chambersburg PA
CBHW070014100426
42741CB00012B/3242